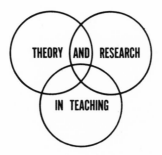

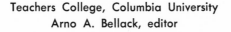

Teachers College, Columbia University
Arno A. Bellack, editor

Recent years have witnessed a resurgence of
interest on the part of educational researchers
in the teaching process. Volumes in the *Theory
and Research in Teaching* series report significant studies of instructional procedures in a
variety of educational settings, at various or-
ganizational levels in the schools, and in many
of the subjects included in the curriculum.
These studies present fresh perspectives on
teaching both to educational researchers and
to practitioners in the schools.

THE INDIVIDUALIZED INSTRUCTION GAME

James L. Neujahr

TEACHERS COLLEGE PRESS

Teachers College, Columbia University
New York and London

Library of Congress Cataloging in Publication Data:

Neujahr, James L.   1939–
   The individualized instruction game.

   (Theory and research in teaching)
   Bibliography: p.
   1. Individualized instruction. I. Title.
II. Series.
LB1031.N39   372.1'39'4   75–22491
ISBN 0–8077–2485–8
ISBN 0–8077–2484–X pbk.

Foreword

A distinctive feature of contemporary research on teaching is emphasis on naturalistic observation and description of teacher-student interaction in regular classroom settings. Most descriptive studies have been undertaken in conventional classrooms, in which the prevailing pattern of instruction is the traditional recitation. Scant attention has been given by researchers to descriptions of classrooms in which teachers have attempted to organize instruction along rather more innovative lines. For example, although many schools report efforts to establish programs of individualized instruction, there have been few studies that provide detailed descriptions of teaching-learning activities in classrooms in which some form of individualization has been introduced. The research by James Neujahr reported in this volume helps us understand what life is like in classrooms in which individualized modes of instruction have replaced the usual recitation.

Dr. Neujahr's study of individualized sixth-grade classes in a suburban middle school is significant on several counts. First, it focuses attention on the interaction of individual boys and girls with their teachers, rather than presenting pupil data in terms of the "average pupil." Second, in contrast with most studies that concentrate solely on verbal aspects of teacher-student activities, this research describes three additional categories of behavior: non-verbal, extra-linguistic, and spacial dimensions of classroom events. Third, since the system of analysis employed in this research has been used in several other classroom investigations, comparison with other studies using the same analytic instrument is facilitated.

Hopefully, this study will stimulate further investigations of what actually happens in classrooms in which innovative teaching methods, such as individualized instruction, are introduced.

Arno A. Bellack

Acknowledgments

There are many who helped make this possible. There are, first, the teachers and kids who put up with videotaping for nearly a month, and did so with good humor. The school's audio-visual specialist helped with all the technical aspects of recording. Second is a group of faculty from Teachers College, Columbia, who gave freely of their time, especially Arno Bellack, George Ivany, Jeremy Kilpatrick, James T. Robinson, and Frank L. Smith. All were instrumental in the first part of my work which resulted in a dissertation.

It is a painful process to go from dissertation to monograph. I took the step only because of the encouragement and support of Arno Bellack. The editorial staff at TC Press, particularly Willa Rosenblatt Speiser, has given much assistance in the rewriting. Finally, my wife Luda has helped all along the way.

I thank you all.

J. N.

Contents

The Individualized
Instruction Game

ONE
The Research Context

In the back corner of the room Peter turned to the next frame on the filmstrip, looked toward the projected image, then began writing. After a slight pause he turned to the following frame and repeated the process. Linda stood, glanced toward the occupied filmstrip corner, then toward the teacher's desk where Mr. Green, the teacher, was talking with a student. She hesitated, then went to the library area and began thumbing through books. Here are two students, each working alone in a sixth-grade social studies class where the teacher is individualizing instruction. All of the students are working on a six-week unit on ancient Rome. A minimum of work has been specified for them in such activities as map work, filmstrip summaries, and biographies. They work at a speed and in a sequence that they choose, and arrange with the teacher for work beyond the minimum. The teacher regularly checks pupil progress.

In a neighboring class Mr. Mandel is slowly circling the room. Students are all working independently at their desks, doing math problems. A brief glance shows they are at different pages in their text. Mr. Mandel looks over John's shoulder, pauses, moves on. He looks toward Mary who is neither reading nor writing, just sitting and looking somewhat troubled. Mr. Mandel goes to her desk. "What's the problem?" They talk for a minute. "Everything clear now?" Mary nods. Mr. Mandel turns and goes to his desk. He scans the room, then begins to correct papers. This is typical of Mr. Mandel's behavior in his version of individualized instruction.

Jim and Steve are talking at their desks. Like their classmates they have been paired off to work on individual research projects on the general subject of conservation. They have gone through the early stages of settling on a question to investigate and are now trying to decide how to get the information they want about food wastage in their school cafeteria. Jim talks rapidly, giving Steve little chance to get in. Steve finally has an opening, points out a problem with the suggested procedure,

1

then is interrupted by another burst from Jim. At his desk Mr. Wells is enquiring about the ways Susan and Carol have considered for measuring the depth of the school pond. Two other pairs are waiting in line to talk with him.

TYPES OF INDIVIDUALIZED INSTRUCTION

The teachers in these three classes varied in their interpretation of individualized instruction. All individualized their attention, interacting primarily with individuals or pairs of students. All individualized the pace at which students worked: students could work as fast or as slowly as was appropriate for them. The differences among the teachers lay in the individualization of content. In Mr. Mandel's math class all students worked with the same text, doing the same problems at different speeds. Mr. Green's students were working within a set of teacher-determined activities in the teacher-determined area of ancient Rome. The activities provided some alternatives and there was considerable freedom in choice of topic for work beyond the minimum. Mr. Wells' students had the greatest freedom of choice, being limited only to projects which came under the heading of conservation.

These are the three contexts examined in this study. The teachers are like many others who approach education without the constraints of a packaged program for individualized instruction. They are teachers who decided together that they wanted to individualize instruction. All three succeeded in individualizing their attention: over eighty percent of their interactions were with one or two pupils. They succeeded to a considerable extent in individualizing the pace at which children worked but varied in the degree to which content was individualized.

Obviously the term "individualized instruction" covers a much broader range of situations than those illustrated here. They range from classes with little structure, as at Summerhill, to the more constrained packaged programs such as Individually Prescribed Instruction (IPI). They range from those having a progressive philosophy and a psychological base resting in Piagetian theory to programs with a behaviorist orientation. As Gibbons [1] noted, there is so much variety in programs of individualized instruction that the label by itself has little meaning.

OBSERVATIONAL RESEARCH

As there are many ways of individualizing instruction, there are also many approaches to observing in the classroom. Chart 1 suggests some

[1] Maurice Gibbons, *Individualized Instruction* (New York: Teachers College Press, 1971), ch. 1.

CHART 1
Dimensions for Observation

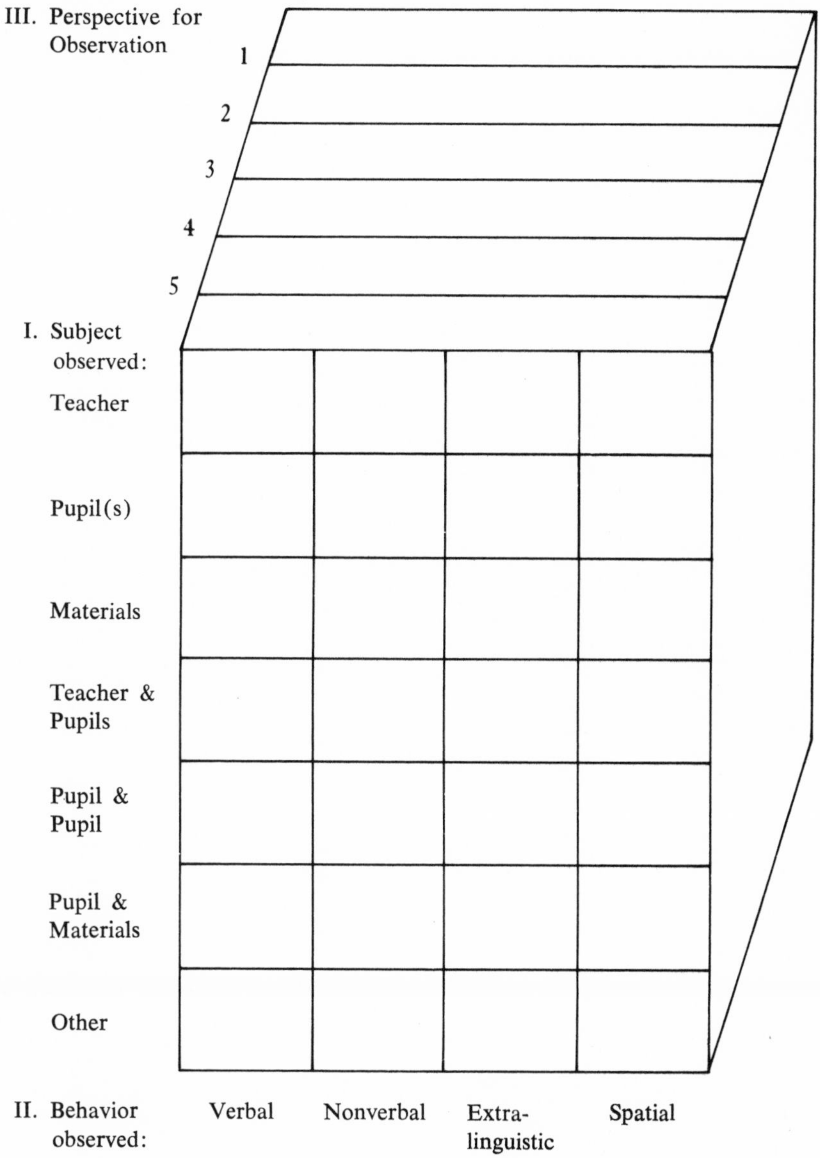

III. Perspective for
    Observation   1
              2
            3
          4
        5

I. Subject
    observed:

    Teacher

    Pupil(s)

    Materials

    Teacher &
    Pupils

    Pupil &
    Pupil

    Pupil &
    Materials

    Other

II. Behavior   Verbal   Nonverbal   Extra-   Spatial
    observed: linguistic

of these. We can focus on the teacher, the pupils, or the materials through which instruction is mediated. Materials include the audiovisual hardware and software, books, laboratory and other manipulative equipment, maps, charts, and so forth. Pupils can be individual pupils, a subset of pupils such as low-achieving boys, or all the pupils in the class as a group. We can also focus on interactions between these such as teacher-pupil, pupil-pupil, or pupil-materials.

A second dimension is that of the behavior to be observed. Weick [2] suggests four categories of behavior: verbal, non-verbal, extra-linguistic, and spatial. Verbal behavior includes not only the talk that occurs, but reading and writing as well. We can study the conversation between Susan, Carol, and Mr. Wells, and in this study we do. We can also study the relationship between the filmstrip text and Peter's notes. Gestures, facial expressions, body movements, and glances are elements of non-verbal behavior. Some researchers have attempted to include in their analysis such behaviors as Mary's look of puzzlement or Linda's glance toward the filmstrip projector. Extra-linguistic behavior has a vocal aspect consisting of pitch, timbre, and loudness; a temporal aspect with rate, duration, and rhythm as components; and interaction aspect which includes interruptions and dominating or inhibiting behaviors; and a stylistic aspect which includes vocabulary and diction. Few observational studies have focused on these extra-linguistic behaviors. Under the spatial category Weick includes movements of pupils and the spatial relationships between them. I include here the spatial organization of objects and areas in the classroom.

To these two dimensions should be added a third, namely the perspective from which one views classroom actors and their behaviors. One investigator may be interested in the way content is handled, another with emotional aspects of interaction, another with health practices of children, another with moral development. It is not surprising that the definitive study of the classroom has not been attempted, nor is it likely to be.

Most classroom studies have focused on teacher-pupil interactions in large group settings. Many of the observational instruments have been developed within a social psychological framework with particular emphasis on leadership behavior. The broad range of research possibilities suggested by Chart 1 has only been sampled. If this is true for whole

    [2] Karl E. Weick, "Systematic Observational Methods," *The Handbook for Social Psychology,* eds. Gardner Lindzey and Elliot Aronson (2nd ed.; Reading, Mass.: Addison-Wesley, 1968), II, 357–451.

class settings, how much more so for studies of individualized instruction where little research has been done.[3] Interestingly, none of the observational research on individualized instruction has kept track of individual pupils; pupil data have always represented an "average pupil." I chose to focus on the interactions of individual pupils with the teacher, paying attention to some of the verbal, non-verbal, and spatial aspects of this interaction.

DESCRIPTION OF THE PROJECT

Mr. Wells, Mr. Green, Mr. Mandel, and an English teacher constituted a team responsible for four sixth-grade classes. Each taught his particular subject to each of the four classes. We spent a week with each teacher, video-taping him with each class. This resulted in approximately 20 periods of video-tape with each teacher and 20 with each class.

The taping was done in the new middle school of a New York City suburb. The school was equipped with extensive audiovisual resources: a library, media center, dial-access television with monitors in each room, and carrels in a commons area also equipped with a monitor and dial access to the media center. In addition there were extensive hilly, wooded grounds used as a science resource. It was in this context that three of the four teachers decided to individualize instruction.

Two remotely operated cameras were used, one focused on the teacher, the other on the class. Pictures were combined in a split screen or corner format. The teacher wore a microphone so that even hushed talk with a quiet pupil was picked up. Other researchers have claimed that after a day or so teachers and pupils forget about the television cameras, and this seemed to be generally true. A few pupils continued

---

[3] There have been a few attempts to study individualized instruction. C. M. Lindvall et al. ("Manual for IPI Student Observational Form," *Mirrors for Behavior*, vol. III, eds. Anita Simon and E. Gil Boyer [Philadelphia: Research for Better Schools Incorporated, 1967]), Dewey Lipe, Margaret T. Steen, and Thomas J. Quirk ("PLAN Student Observation Scale," *Mirrors for Behavior*, vol. B), and Fred K. Honigan and James Stephens ("Student Activity Profile," *Mirrors for Behavior*, vol. X) developed check lists for sampling pupil behavior in IPI, Project PLAN, and Learning Activity Packages settings, respectively. They observed all pupils, checking the activity of one, then moving on to another, until the activity of all had been sampled. The resulting picture is of the "average pupil." Margaret T. Steen, Thomas J. Quirk, and Dewey Lipe ("PLAN Teacher Observational Scale," *Mirrors for Behavior*, vol. B) developed a check list to categorize teacher behaviors in Project PLAN classes, but without attention to the particular pupils the teacher interacted with. Lauren B. Resnick ("Teacher Behavior in an Informal British Infant School," *School Review*, Nov., 1972) categorized utterances of teachers in English infant schools, but also did not keep track of the individual pupils involved.

to react overtly to the cameras, but the teachers assured us that had the cameras not been there, these pupils would have found something else to distract them from their work.

The pupils were streamed in the four classes according to teacher assessment of their ability. The coding system described in the next chapter was developed using tapes of the two lower ability classes. The data reported in Chapters 3 through 6 are from the most able of the four classes. For this group, technical problems rendered one of the social studies tapes unusable. The data reported are from two one-hour periods and one 40-minute period. Five 40-minute periods were recorded in mathematics and science. For two of the mathematics periods the teacher reverted to whole-class instruction. Although this was completely un-anticipated, it provided an opportunity to compare teacher and pupil behavior in two instructional settings in the same week.

TWO
The Observational System

When observing in classrooms the researcher has the option of devising his own analytic categories or of using some form of an existing observational instrument. I chose the latter, a choice which facilitates comparisons with other studies using the same instrument. The system selected was that devised by Bellack.[1] It was modified for the individualized context as well as for coding non-verbal and spatial aspects of interaction. The basic unit of Bellack's system, the move, gives a picture of the roles played in the interactive context. It gives equal emphasis to both teacher and pupil communications. As a unit the move lends itself to a fine analysis of the content of communications. In the first part of this chapter we will look at the rationale for Bellack's system and for the modifications I made in it. Then the actual coding categories and examples are presented.

AN OVERVIEW OF THE OBSERVATIONAL SYSTEM

Bellack's *The Language of the Classroom* is a study of the various types of meaning communicated through speaking. In that book the communication of meaning was assumed to be the primary function of language. The meaning of an utterance was understood in much the same way as the meaning of a word was for Wittgenstein: meaning was tied to the use of the utterance in discourse. Bellack was again influenced by Wittgenstein in his conceptualization of the verbal activity in a classroom as a game participated in by players according to a set of usually unspecified rules. The language game metaphor "suggested a framework of analysis within which we could identify verbal expressions that communicated various kinds of meaning." [2]

The basic unit of analysis is the pedagogical move, a verbal activity

---

[1] Arno Bellack, Herbert M. Kleibard, Ronald T. Hyman, and Frank L. Smith, Jr., *The Language of the Classroom* (New York: Teachers College Press, 1966).
[2] *Ibid.*, pp. 3, 4.

which performs a function within the classroom game. Four basic functions, and thus four moves, were identified: structuring, soliciting, responding, and reacting. Structuring moves set the context for interaction. Soliciting moves call for another to make a response. Responding moves fulfill the expectation of soliciting moves. Reacting moves are occasioned by structuring, soliciting, responding, or other reacting moves, but they are not directly elicited. Reacting moves often serve to rate a previous move. The first step in analysis is to determine the type of move being made and its boundaries.

Next Bellack looked at the meaning being expressed through the move. He dichotomized meaning: it was either substantive (having to do with subject matter) or instructional (dealing with assignments, materials, procedures, personal remarks, and so forth). If a move had substantive meaning, it was coded according to the particular type of substantive meaning. In addition it was coded according to the type of logical process used in communicating the substantive meaning. Logical processes included defining, explaining, justifying, fact stating, interpreting, and opining. If the move had instructional meaning, it was coded according to the type of instructional meaning as well as the logical process used in expressing this meaning. On occasion a single move conveyed both substantive and instructional meanings, and was coded in all categories.

The Modified System

The move. The analysis began with identification of the pedagogical moves in the interaction between teacher and pupil—structuring, soliciting, responding, and reacting moves. In the initial viewing of the video-tapes I found that these functions were often effected through means other than speaking. Thus the move was conceptualized as having a form. The form could be oral and verbal as in speaking, oral and non-verbal as in sounds such as "ughhh!", non-oral and verbal as in writing, and non-oral and non-verbal as in gestures. Meanings could also be expressed through combinations of these forms. The opportunity to analyze the form of the move developed from using video-tapes rather than audio-tapes. The video-tapes also made it clear which pupils were interacting with the teacher. Since individualized instruction is an attempt to recognize the differences between individual students, these individual differences should show up in an analysis of individualized instruction. Instead of using a general category for any pupil who made a move, I coded the particular emitter of each move. The moves a pupil makes generally represent less than half of his interaction with a teacher. What the teacher says represents the rest. Thus I added a target dimension to the coding system in which individual targets (up to four in number) of a teacher's moves were identified.

The context. Two other dimensions were added to Bellack's system, allowing it to account for ecological or context kinds of variables. Here context variables are the size of the communication group and the location of this group. The communication group is composed of those pupils with whom the teacher is intentionally interacting. In terms of the game metaphor, these dimensions were added to explore whether the game between the teacher and one pupil differed from that played with larger groups, or whether the game played at the teacher's desk differed, for example, from that played at a media location. After determining the boundaries of a move, it was coded as to the type of move, its form, the emitter and target, and the group size and location. The meaning conveyed through the move was coded last.

The content. I followed Bellack in coding a move for its substantive and substantive logical or instructional and instructional logical meanings. Substantive meaning was coded only in terms of relevance to the particular subject area. When a move focused on subject matter, either by requesting or giving it, it was coded in the substantive meaning and substantive logical meaning categories.

If the move focused on areas other than subject matter, for example, assignments, materials, procedures, or activities, it was coded in the appropriate instructional meaning category and instructional logical meaning category. Again, Bellack's categories were in general followed. In the preliminary analysis of the video-tapes I subdivided some of the instructional meaning categories. They have been collapsed again to make the data reported here comparable to that reported for other studies.[3] A few modifications remain in the instructional logical categories. Bellack's six rating categories are collapsed into three: positive, negative, and qualifying. Because of the large number of directives given and requested, the extra-logical categories were expanded to account for different types of directives as well as moves which satisfied directives. Chart 2 shows the major dimensions of the coding system.

The dimensions of Chart 2 and the categories in the summary at the end of this chapter are evidence of the ways the move, as a unit, lends itself to fine analysis. The move also lends itself to being gathered

---

[3] For the full elaboration of instructional meaning categories and data on the subcategories see James L. Neujahr, "An Analysis of Teacher-Pupil Interactions when Instruction Is Individualized" (unpublished Ed.D. dissertation, Teachers College, Columbia University, 1970).

CHART 2

The Dimensions of the Coding System

 I. The Pedagogical Move

   A. Move type: the function served by a move.
   B. Move form: the way in which the move is made.
   C. Emitter: the particular person or persons making a move.
   D. Target: the particular person or persons to whom a move is directed.

 II. The Context of Teacher-Pupil Interaction

   A. Group size: the number of pupils involved with the teacher.
   B. Group location: the place where teacher-pupil interaction occurs.

III. The Content of the Move

   A. Substantive meaning: the type of subject matter conveyed or requested in the move.
   B. Substantive logical meaning: the type of logical process used in making a move with substantive meaning.
   C. Instructional meaning: the type of nonsubstantive information conveyed or requested in the move.
   D. Instructional logical meaning: the type of logical process used in making a move with instructional meaning.

---

into larger units. (Bellack did this by constructing cycles.) A unit which is particularly significant for the present study is one composed of all the communication between the teacher and a given pupil or pupils at a given time. This is called an interaction unit. It begins with the first move in a particular grouping of teacher and pupils and usually ends with the move prior to any change in the composition of this group. Exceptions are in the case of (1) an interruption, where the continuation of inter-action after the interruption is considered to be part of the unit initiated before the interruption, and (2) a change in some, not all, of the pupil participants where there is no accompanying change in the focus of interaction. The interaction unit may consist of one move or many moves. It is the primary subgame in the individualized instruction setting.

THE SYSTEM OF ANALYSIS

The categories used to analyze classes where instruction is individualized are presented in this section. Many of these also occur in *The Language of the Classroom*. As far as possible, the definitions of common categories are those developed in Bellack's project. Coding procedures and the reliability study are presented in the last section of this chapter. Specific coding instructions are given in the Appendix.

The Pedagogical Move

Move type. Pedagogical moves are the basic units of classroom communication. They described the interactions of teachers and pupils in the classroom. Four basic types of moves characterize the interplay of teachers and pupils: structuring and soliciting, which are initiatory moves; and responding and reacting, which are reflexive moves.

(1) *"Structuring* (STR). Structuring moves serve the function of setting the context for subsequent behavior by (1) launching or halting-excluding interactions between teacher and pupils, and (2) indicating the nature of the interaction in terms of the dimensions of time, agent, activity, location, objects involved, and cognitive processes. A structuring move may set the context for the entire classroom game or a part of the game. . . . Structuring moves do not elicit a response, are not in themselves direct responses, and are not called out by anything in the immediate classroom situation except the speaker's concept of what should be said or taught." [4]

Examples:
T: In a few minutes I'll be coming around to look at your work. If I have any questions, I'll ask you about it.
T: Before starting work today, I'd like to spend a few minutes discussing what has been happening in Vietnam.
T: There are about five minutes left.

(2) *"Soliciting* (SOL). Moves in this category are intended to elicit (a) an active verbal response on the part of the person addressed; (b) a cognitive response, e.g., encouraging persons addressed to attend to something; or (c) a physical response. . . . Although these moves may take all grammatical forms—declarative, interrogative, and imperative—the interrogative occurs most frequently. In coding soliciting moves, the various categories of analysis are coded in terms of the response expected rather than the solicitation itself." [5]

Examples:
T: John, bring your folder up here.
P: Where are the pencils?
T: Which problem are you working on?

[4] Bellack *et al., The Language of the Classroom,* pp. 16, 17.
[5] *Ibid.,* p. 18.

(3) *"Responding* (RES). Responding moves bear a reciprocal relationship to soliciting moves and occur only in relation to them. Their pedagogical function is to fulfill the expectation of soliciting moves and is, therefore, reflexive in nature. Since solicitations and responses are defined in relationship to each other, there can be no solicitation that is not intended to elicit a response, and no response that has not been directly elicited by a solicitation." [6]

Examples:
P: (John brings his folder to the teacher)
T: We don't have any more. They've all been taken.
P: I'm working on this one (points).

(4) *"Reacting* (REA). These moves are *occasioned* by a structuring, soliciting, responding, or a prior reacting move, but are not directly elicited by them. Pedagogically, these moves serve to modify (by clarifying, synthesizing, or expanding) and/or to rate (positively or negatively) what was said [or done] in the move(s) that occasioned them. Reacting moves differ from responding moves: while a responding move is always directly elicited by a solicitation, *preceding moves serve only as the occasion for reactions."* [7]

Examples:
T: You're on the right track.
T: That's a good question.
T: I guessed that you hadn't finished it.

(5) *Not codable* (NOC). Pedagogical function is uncertain because the tape is inaudible.[8]

The move form. Meanings are communicated in the classroom in several different ways. The pedagogical move may have oral or non-oral forms, each of which may be verbal or non-verbal. The move may also be expressed through a combination of these forms.

(1) *Speaking* (SPK). The cognitive meanings are fully expressed through oral and verbal activity, including discourse and reading aloud.

(2) *Sound* (SND). A cognitive meaning is expressed through an oral and non-verbal mode. This includes laughter, groaning, or other noises of human or non-human origin when they serve a pedagogical function.

---

[6] *Ibid.,* p. 18.
[7] *Ibid.,* pp. 18, 19.
[8] *Ibid.,* p. 38.

(3) *Writing* (WRI). The cognitive meanings are communicated through the writing of words or other symbols with no accompanying talk, or through reading these symbols.

(4) *Gesturing* (GES). The cognitive meaning is communicated through gesture alone. This includes pointing to indicated location, to exhibit, to denote; directing gestures which control movement, vocal actions, and so forth; gestures such as "I don't know" shrugs; and manipulation of an object or objects to reveal something about the objects themselves or to illustrate some concept.

(5) *Speaking and writing* (S/W). The cognitive meaning is communicated both through speaking and through writing.

(6) *Speaking and gesturing* (S/G). The cognitive meaning is communicated in part through speaking, in part through gesturing.

Emitter. The emitter is the person or object that utters the sound or makes the gesture that performs the pedagogical function. The emitter is the source of the move.

(1) *Individual emitter* (a different number is assigned to each pupil and teacher). One person makes the move. His identity is specified if known. Otherwise the emitter is coded as "uncertain."

(2) *Multiple emitters* (M). More than one person emits the move.

(3) *Audiovisual device* (A/V). An audiovisual device is the emitter of the move.

Target. The target consists of those to whom the move is directed, i.e. those who are expected to attend to the move. When there are four or fewer people to whom a move is directed, these people are individually identified.

The Context of Teacher-Pupil Interaction

Group size. The communication group is that group of pupils with whom a teacher is intentionally in communication for a particular move. Since we are studying teacher-pupil interactions, the teacher is always assumed to be a member of the communication group, but he is not counted in establishing group size.

The communication group is coded as having one, two, three, four, more than four, or an uncertain number of pupil participants. These are the group size categories.

Group location. The group location is the physical setting of the communication group for a particular move. The teacher may not be in the same location as the pupils with whom he is in communication.

If there are pupils outside the communication group who are closer to the teacher than any of the pupils with whom he is in communication, the communication group is considered separated.

(1) *Uncertain* (UNC). The location of the group is uncertain because it is out of camera range.

(2) *Classroom* (CLR). The group members are dispersed throughout the classroom.

(3 *Teacher's desk* (DKT). The group members and the teacher are at the teacher's desk.

(4) *Pupil's desk* (DKP). The group members and the teacher are at the desk or table of one of the pupils in the group.

(5) *Media location* (MED). The group members and the teacher are at a projector, wall map, globe, blackboard, model or other piece of apparatus. When the media is at the teacher's or pupil's desk, MED is coded preferentially over DKT or DKP.

(6) *Other location* (OTH). The group is at a localized setting in the classroom other than DKT, DKP, or MED.

(7) *Teacher and pupils separated* (SEP). Other pupils are closer to the teacher than those with whom he is in communication.

The Content of the Move

Substantive meanings. Substantive meanings are coded for those moves or segments of moves in which one is communicating subject matter or soliciting another to communicate certain subject matter. Communications about the subject matter—for example, whether it is hard or easy, whether one understands it or not, and assignments associated with it—are considered to have instructional meaning since they do not contribute directly to the pupil's or teacher's knowledge of the subject nor do they call upon the pupil or teacher to use or demonstrate the knowledge he has on the subject.

(1) *Not coded* (NOC). There is no substantive meaning in the move.

(2) *Relevant to the subject area* (REL). The subject matter being communicated is relevant to the course in general. For instance, in social studies talk about the unit and about current events would both be relevant.

Examples:
T: Which primaries are being held today?
P: Indiana and Nebraska.
T: Define myth.

(3) *Not relevant to the subject area* (NRL). The subject matter being communicated is not relevant to the course in which it is being communicated. A discussion of the nature of solder and its uses, prompted by a pupil having it in his mouth, is considered to be not relevant to social studies.

Example:
T: It's made of lead and tin, and lead is very poisonous.

Substantive logical meanings. Substantive logical meanings refer to the cognitive processes used in communicating the subject matter.

(1) *Defining* (DEF). "To define . . . is to refer to the objects (abstract or concrete) to which the term is applicable. . . . [and/or] to give the set of properties or characteristics that an object (abstract or concrete) must have for the term to be applicable." [9]

Examples:
T: What kind of pulley is this?
P: A moveable pulley.
T: What is a myth?
P: A myth is something like a fairy tale.

(2) "*Interpreting* (INT). To interpret a statement is to give its . . . equivalent, usually for the purpose of rendering its meaning clear." [10] "Interpreting bears the same relationship to statements that defining does to terms." [11]

Examples:
T: Reword the law of levers so that it applies to pulleys.
T: What is another way to say 10 divided by 2?
P: 10 times ½.

(3) *Fact-stating* (FAC). To state a fact is to describe, to report, or to give an account of an object, event, action, or state of affairs, such report, description, or accounting being empirically verifiable at least in theory. Fact-stating is also giving information which is verified analytically, but which may have its truth illustrated empirically, as with arithmetic "facts."

Examples:
T: What does poison ivy look like?
P: It has three shiny green leaves.

[9] *Ibid.*, p. 23.
[10] *Ibid.*, p. 23.
[11] *Ibid.*, p. 22.

T: What is one-third of 60?

P: 20.

(4) *"Explaining* (XPL). To explain is to relate an object, event, action, or state of affairs to some other object, event, action, or state of affairs; or to show the relation between an event or state of affairs and a principle or generalization; or to state the relationships between principles or generalizations." [12]

The relationships may be causal, mechanical, sequential, procedural, teleological, or normative. The relationships must be either (a) empirically verifiable, at least in principle, or (b) analytically verifiable but capable of being illustrated empirically.

Examples:

P: How do you do this problem?

T: In what way is the pulley similar to the lever?

(5) *"Opining* (OPN). To opine is to make statements in which the speaker gives his own valuation regarding (a) what should or ought to be done, or (b) fairness, worth, importance, or quality of an action, event, person, idea, plan, or policy." [13]

Examples:

P: I don't think it's right to name months after emperors.

T: Do you think it's likely that they'd use the Vatican [for peace talks]?

P: No.

(6) *"Justifying* (JUS). To justify is to give *reasons* for holding an opinion regarding (a) what should or ought to be done, or (b) fairness, worth, importance, or quality of an action, event, policy, idea, plan, or thing.

"Justifying statements are intended as support or criticism of opinions that either have been explicit in a previous statement or are implied within the context of the interaction. Justifying statements are frequently preceded by an opining statement, although this is not a necessary condition for coding JUS." [14]

Examples:

T: Why do you think they shouldn't have done that?

T: Why aren't they likely to settle on the Vatican?

[12] *Ibid.,* p. 24.
[13] *Ibid.,* p. 25.
[14] *Ibid.,* p. 26.

(7) *Not clear* (NCL). The logical process being used is not clear.
Instructional meanings. Teacher-pupil communication which focuses upon classroom management, assignments and the work which follows them, classroom activities, or the materials of instruction is coded as having instructional meaning. Instructional meaning is coded in the following categories.

(1) *Statement* (STA). Reference to any utterance or physical gesture, particularly the meaning, validity, truth, or propriety of the utterance or gesture. The utterance may consist of a sound, word, or several paragraphs. The physical gesture may be any that takes the place of an utterance.

Examples:
T: That's right. (Reacting to a verbal response.)
T: O.K.   (Reacting to a non-verbal response.)
P: O.K.   (Responding to a teacher directive.)

(2) *"Logical process* (LOG). Discussion of the way language is used or of a logical process. Includes references to definitions, explanations, reasoning, arguments, and the like." [15]

Examples:
T: You are contradicting yourself.
T: What do I mean when I say to define something?

(3) *Assignment* (ASG). Reference to pupil work which is to be done, in progress, or completed. Includes talk about an assignment, about an answer to a problem or question, about a report or other product of pupil assignment oriented activity, about progress being made, and about evaluation of a pupil's work.

Examples:
T: What kind of assignments do you prefer?
P: Is this the right answer?
T: What are you planning to do after this?
P: I though I'd do a report on Cincinnatus.

(4) *Materials* (MAT). References to materials such as books, audiovisual hardware and software, supplies, or classroom apparatus.

Examples:
P: I don't have my book.
T: I have a camera if anyone needs it.
P: We're looking for a map of Europe.

[15] *Ibid.,* p. 28.

(5) *Procedure* (PRC). Discussion of a course of action or set of activities. Includes references to the way the class is conducted, regulations governing class members, and steps in carrying out work.

Examples:
T: Who is the next to see me after Bill?
T: Only five will be able to go to the library today.
P: We don't know how you focus this.

(6) *"Person* (PER). Discussion of teacher's or pupil's person, physiognomy, dress, expression, or appearance. Used also when a personal experience is the topic under discussion." [16]

Examples:
T: What kind of a pin is that?
T: Do you have spring fever?
P: I go to the movies every week.

(7) *"Action-vocal* (ACV). Reference to action involving the emission of speech or sound. Used for the physical qualities of the action or the act of saying something. This includes references to . . . the pace, volume, pitch, and diction of vocal action." [17]

Examples:
T: You are talking too fast.
T: That sounds like a Boston accent.

(8) *"Action-physical* (ACP). Reference to action where physical movements are primary. Includes writing, passing papers, walking, hearing, and seeing." [18]

Examples:
T: Have you checked your locker?
T: How many are going outside today?

(9) *"Action-cognitive* (ACC). Reference to action where a cognitive process is principally involved. This includes thinking, imagining, knowing, supposing, understanding or not understanding, listening, believing, and reading. . . ." [19]

Examples:
T: Do you know how to divide?

[16] *Ibid.,* p. 27.
[17] *Ibid.,* p. 28.
[18] *Ibid.*
[19] *Ibid.*

P: I don't know.

T: You seem to have forgotten everything.

(10) *"Action-emotional* (ACE). Reference to action where feelings or emotions are principally involved. Includes feeling bad, good, sorry, thankful, grateful, relieved, or upset." [20]

Examples:

T: What are you worried about?

T: I'm sorry I took so long.

T: Thank you, Barton.

(11) *"Action-general* (ACT). Reference to performance, action, or event where the nature of the performance (whether vocal, non-vocal, cognitive, or emotional) can not be determined or when more than one of the sub-categories 7 through 10 are involved." [21]

Examples:

T: What have you been doing?

P: We were working on our check dam, then talking with Mrs. M.

(12) *"Language mechanics* (LAM). Discussion of language usage or grammar." [22]

Examples:

P: How do you say that?

T: Well, how do you say "A – p?"

P: How do you spell vestal?

Instructional logical and extra-logical meanings. Instructional logical meanings include those logical processes listed under substantive logical meanings, as well as the specific type of evaluative process involved in giving positive or negative ratings. Instructional moves with extra-logical meanings are those that cannot be verified by analytic, empirical, or evaluative criteria. Rather than making assertions or denials, these moves make prescriptions or prohibitions, or request that prescriptions or prohibitions be made. Logical meanings are represented as follows:

(1) *Defining* (DEF). Same as in substantive logical meanings.

(2) *Interpreting* (INT). Same as in substantive logical meanings.

(3) *Fact-stating* (FAC). Same as in substantive logical meanings.

(4) *Explaining* (XPL). Same as in substantive logical meanings.

[20] *Ibid.,* p. 29.
[21] *Ibid.,* p. 28.
[22] *Ibid.,* p. 29.

(5) *Opining* (OPN). Same as in substantive logical meanings.

(6) *Justifying* (JUS). Same as in substantive logical meanings.

(7) *Not clear* (NCL). The logical process being used is not clear.

Ratings. Ratings can convey critical and/or evaluative meanings. A critical rating is a judgment of truth or falsity based on rational criteria. An evaluative rating gives the rater's partiality, thus it is a more subjective response. Ratings range from positive to negative. They often occur in reaction to a statement.

(1) *Positive* (POS). Positive ratings range from distinctly affirmative to those that implicitly affirm by repeating what is rated.

Examples:

T: Very good.

T: All right.

T: O.K.

(2) *Qualifying* (QAL). "Any indication of reservation, however mild or oblique, usually in reactions to statements." [23]

Examples:

T: Well, O.K., but there are better ways of doing it.

T: You're right up to this point.

(3) *Negative* (NEG). Negative ratings include those which reject by stating the contrary and those which reject by a distinctly negative rating.

Examples:

T: No, that's not it.

P: That should be 22, not 24.

(4) "*Positive or negative* (PON). Solicitations in which a request is made for either a positive or a negative rating." [24]

Examples:

P: Is this one right?

P: How do you like the way I've done this?

Extra-logical meanings. Three types of extra-logical processes are represented in the extra-logical categories: giving a directive, requesting a directive, and responding to a directive. A directive is given in those moves in which the emitter commands, exhorts, orders, suggests that, requests, advises, or instructs the agent to perform some physical or

---

[23] *Ibid.*, p. 30.
[24] *Ibid.*, p. 31.

cognitive act. Pupils often request a directive or permission to do something. The move that is expected to follow this move is a solicitation in which a particular activity is prescribed, permitted, or prohibited. The third type of extra-logical process is reflexive rather than initiatory. These categories are coded for behavior that carries out or indicates intention to carry out or not carry out a directive.

(1) *Prescribing a performance* (PRE). The agent is directed to carry out the activity. The action is not optional.

Examples:
T: You need to get another report in.
P: (Hands the teacher a paper and points to where the teacher is to begin reading.)

(2) *Permitting a performance* (PER). The agent is allowed to carry out the activity. The performance is optional. A move coded PER often follows a move seeking permission.

Example:
T: Yes, you may (get a drink, go to the library, etc.).

(3) *Prohibiting a performance* (PRO). The agent is directed to cease, or not to embark upon, a particular activity.

Examples:
T: O.K., I've had enough of all this talking.
T: Get your feet off the wall, Frank.

(4) *Prescribing a repetition* (RPT). The agent is directed to repeat the communication.

Examples:
T: Pardon?
P: What was that?

(5) *Asking to be directed* (DIR). The emitter of this move is trying to find out what he is or is not to do. He expects to be given a directive. His solicitation may be general, involve several alternatives, or only one.

Examples:
P: What should I do next, Mr. Y?
P: Are we supposed to do number 4?

(6) *Seeking permission* (RPR). The emitter of this move is requesting that he be permitted to perform a particular activity.

Examples:
P: May I get a drink?
P: May I go to the library now?

(7) *Compliance* (COM). The person to whom a directive is addressed either begins to carry out the directive or indicates that he intends to carry it out.

Examples:
P: (Closes door in response to teacher directive to do so.)
P: O.K. (in response to teacher directive to study more).

(8) *Alternative* (ALT). The person to whom a directive is addressed indicates that he will carry out some activity in place of the one prescribed, or that he will carry out the prescribed activity at other than the prescribed time.

Example:
P: I'll put it in my pocket (in response to a teacher directive to give him a piece of solder).

(9) *Non-compliance* (NCM). The person to whom a directive is addressed indicates that he will not perform a prescribed activity and he gives no alternative.

Example:
P: I can't. It's not mine (in response to a teacher directive to give him a clicker).

CODING AND RELIABILITY

Category abbreviations have been included in the presentation of the system of analysis because they are useful in presenting tables of data. The actual coding was all numerical and was done on IBM tabulation sheets, facilitating the subsequent transfer of data to cards for computer processing. Coding was carried out as follows. Because of the complexity of the system, a typescript was made from the video-tape. Both typescript and video-tape were referred to when coding. A page of typescript was read, tentatively divided into moves, and coding uncertainties noted. Then the video-tape for that page was observed. This was followed by coding in all categories with replay of the video-tape when necessary. Coding began with the move and the emitter. Next the context categories were coded; they usually remained constant for several moves. Finally the substantive and/or instructional categories were coded. The maximum coding was of about 80 moves per hour. All coding was done by this investigator, after determining the reliability of my coding.

For the reliability study, a sample of five percent of the data to be used was coded independently by two trained coders and myself. The coders, prior to training, had some knowledge of Bellack's system for analysis as well as of the types of modifications of that system made in the present study. One of the coders participated in Bellack's original study. Thus comparability of the coding in that study and in this study was assured. Training consisted of three sessions totaling approximately ten hours during which the system was explained, coded typescripts studied, and other typescripts coded. The three coders agreed in the coding of 94 percent of all moves, that is, we agreed on the boundaries of the move and the type of move. Given agreement in the coding of move type, we agreed in the further analysis of the move (context and content dimensions) between 90 percent and 100 percent of the time. The remarkably high percentage of agreement between independent coders in coding the move indicates that the move is a reliable basic unit for analyzing communication in the classroom.

SUMMARY OF THE CODING SYSTEM

I. The Pedagogical Move

   A. Move Type
     1. Structuring (STR): sets the context for interaction by launching or halting—excluding behavior '
     2. Soliciting (SOL): directly elicits verbal, physical, or mental response
     3. Responding (RES): fulfills expectation of soliciting move
     4. Reacting (REA): occasioned, but not directly elicited, by a previous move which it modifies or rates

   B. Move Form
     1. Speaking (SPK): meaning expressed through oral-verbal activity
     2. Sound (SND): meaning expressed through oral-non-verbal activity
     3. Writing (WRI): meaning expressed completely through written words and symbols; non-oral-verbal
     4. Gesturing (GES): meaning expressed through gesture alone; non-oral-non-verbal

5. Speaking and writing (S/W): part of the meaning of the move is communicated through speaking, part through writing

6. Speaking and gesturing (S/G): meaning is communicated in part through speaking, in part through gesturing

C. Emitter
1. Individual (each assigned a number): one person makes the move
2. Multiple (M): more than one person emits the move
3. Audiovisual device (A/V): an audiovisual device emits the move

D. Target
When a move is directed to four or fewer people, the identity of each is coded

II. The Context of Teacher-Pupil Interaction

A. Group Size
The group is coded as having one, two, three, four, more than four, or an uncertain number of pupil participants (1, 2, 3, 4, 5+, or U)

B. Group Location
1. Uncertain (UNC): group location is uncertain
2. Classroom (CLR): group members dispersed throughout room
3. Teacher's desk (DKT): teacher and pupil(s) at teacher's desk
4. Pupil's desk (DKP): teacher and pupil(s) at the desk of a pupil in the group
5. Media location (MED): teacher and pupil(s) are at a media (educational equipment) location
6. Other location (OTH): the teacher and pupil(s) are at a localized setting other than DKT, DKP, or MED
7. Teacher and pupil separated (SEP): other pupils are closer to the teacher than those with whom he is communicating

III. The Content of the Move

A. Substantive Meaning
1. Not coded (NOC): there is no substantive meaning
2. Relevant to subject area (REL): subject matter com-

municated in the move is relevant to the course in general
3. Not relevant to subject area (NRL): subject matter is not relevant to the course in which it is being communicated

B. Substantive Logical Meaning
1. Defining (DEF): reference to that which is denoted by a term, and/or giving characteristics an object must have for the term to be applicable
2. Interpreting (INT): verbal equivalence of a statement
3. Fact stating (FAC): describe, report, or give an account of an object, event, action, or state of affairs
4. Explaining (XPL): relate an object, event, action, or state of affairs to some other object, event, action, or state of affairs
5. Opining (OPN): make a value statement in which emitter's own values are only criteria
6. Justifying (JUS): reasons or arguments for or against an opinion or judgment
7. Not clear (NCL): the logical process being used is not clear

C. Instructional Meaning
1. Statement (STA): verbal utterance or gesture, particularly its meaning, validity, truth, propriety
2. Logical process (LOG): reference to use of language or logical process
3. Assignment (ASG): reference to pupil work which is to be done, in progress, or completed
4. Materials (MAT): teaching aids and instructional supplies, equipment
5. Procedure (PRC): a plan of activities or a course of action
6. Person (PER): person as physical object, personal appearance, personal experience
7. Action-vocal (ACV): physical qualities of vocal action
8. Action-physical (ACP): physical movement or process
9. Action-cognitive (ACC): action where cognitive process principally involved; thinking, knowing, and so forth
10. Action-emotional (ACE): emotion or feeling; not the expression of an attitude or value
11. Action-general (ACT): a performance, the specific nature of which is uncertain or complex
12. Language mechanics (LAM): rules of grammar or usage

D. Instructional-Logical Meaning

Logical meanings
1. Defining (DEF): (same as substantive-logical)
2. Interpreting (INT): (same as substantive-logical)
3. Fact stating (FAC): (same as substantive-logical)
4. Explaining (XPL): (same as substantive-logical)
5. Opining (OPN): (same as substantive-logical)
6. Justifying (JUS): (same as substantive-logical)
7. Not clear (NCL): (same as substantive-logical)

Ratings
1. Positive (POS): ratings ranging from implicitly positive to distinctly positive
2. Qualifying (QAL): rating in which reservation is expressed
3. Negative (NEG): distinctly negative rating
4. Positive or negative (PON): solicitations in which request is made for a rating

Extralogical meanings
1. Prescribing a performance (PRE): agent directed to carry out the activity
2. Permitting a performance (PER): agent allowed to carry out the activity
3. Prohibiting a performance (PRO): agent directed to cease or not begin an activity
4. Prescribing a repetition (RPT): agent directed to repeat his communication
5. Asking to be directed (DIR): emitter requests a directive
6. Seeking permission (RPR): emitter requests permission to perform an activity
7. Compliance (COM): target of a directive begins to carry out activity or indicates intention to do so
8. Alternative (ALT): target of directive indicates a substitute activity he will carry out
9. Non-compliance (NCM): target of directive indicates he will not carry out the directive

THREE
The Data:
The Context of the Move

The background has been sketched, the glasses through which we are looking described. What picture emerges of the individualized classes, their teachers and pupils? On the most general level the picture is fairly similar across subject areas. The teacher is the most active participant and makes the greater number of initiating and reacting moves. Pupils do the most responding. The classes are distinguished from lecture discussion classes by the smaller differences between roles of teachers and pupils. As the activities are viewed more and more closely, similarities tend to be replaced by notable differences. These include differences in the way boys and girls play the game and differences in the way individual pupils play the game.

The data from these classes are presented here by category. The data from each category are given first in terms of the teacher and all pupils, that is, the activity is that of the teacher and a "generalized" pupil. Comparisons are made between these data and those for lecture-discussion classes. Data are then examined in terms of the average boy and the average girl. Finally, where appropriate, data on the same category of behavior are examined for individual pupils. After this consideration of each category of behavior, interactions of various categories, such as the location in which a communication is made and the content of that communication, will be analyzed. In this chapter we look at the data relating to the context in which behavior occurs. The following chapters will report data related to the form and function of behavior, and to the content communicated.

THE CONTEXT OF THE MOVE

Interaction between teachers and pupils takes place in groups of various size, located in various classroom areas. Group size and location represent the two dimensions for describing the context of the move.

Group Size

Teacher and pupils. Looking at the number of pupils in communication with the teacher provides information on the nature of that class. In all classes but classes 4 and 5,[1] the teachers claimed to be individualizing instruction. Since the major common element in these teachers' conceptions of individualized instruction was the small group or individual interactions of the teacher, a reasonable measure of the degree to which classes were individualized is the percentage of moves made with an individual or small group of pupils. Arbitrarily considering four or fewer pupils with the teacher as a small group, we found at least two-thirds of the moves in each class that the teacher claimed to be individualizing were made in a small group (see Table 1). In classes 4 and 5 less than two percent [2] of the moves were made in small groups. Over 98 percent involved the teacher and a majority of the students in the class. Future references to the lecture-discussion classes of this study refer to classes 4 and 5. The other classes are considered individualized. In this study "individualized" is applied to classes in which the majority of teacher-pupil interactions take place with four or fewer pupils involved with the teacher.

The amount of large group interaction in the individualized classes varied. In two of the social studies classes (6 and 7) the period began with a discussion of current events. Following this the pupils turned to their individualized work on ancient Rome. During one of the science classes (9) the whole class was doing an experiment preceded by extensive procedural comments to the class and followed by class discussion of the results. In the other classes the teacher interaction with the entire class centered on such matters as assignments and procedures.

Boys, girls, and teacher. Slicing the individualized instruction data along subject areas rather than each class session, and looking at the size of group in which the average boy and average girl interacts, we get the results presented in Table 2.

For both boys and girls some generalizations can be made. Both were interacting alone or with one other pupil in at least 80 percent of their interactions with the teacher, regardless of subject area. In mathematics and social studies most of the interaction involved just one pupil. In science many more of the interactions involved two pupils

---

[1] In the tables, classes numbered 1 through 5 are mathematics classes; classes numbered 6 through 8 are social studies classes; and classes numbered 9 through 13 are science classes.

[2] In the tables percentages are carried to tenths of a percent. In the text they are rounded off to the nearest whole percent.

TABLE 1

Distribution of Moves in Communication Groups of Various Sizes

| | Percent of Moves | | | | | f |
| | Number of Pupils With the Teacher | | | | | |
Class	1	2	3	4	5+	
1	84.6	6.0	0.2	0.2	8.7	807
2	75.9	4.5	0.0	0.0	19.2	570
3	74.8	0.0	0.0	0.0	25.1	398
4	1.2	0.0	0.0	0.0	98.7	822
5	0.0	0.0	0.0	0.0	100.0	730
6	65.2	14.2	5.0	0.0	15.6	500
7	64.2	8.6	7.0	1.7	18.2	509
8	88.9	6.0	1.0	0.0	3.9	659
9	14.8	50.7	0.1	2.2	31.9	532
10	46.0	43.9	0.2	0.0	9.7	441
11	13.7	75.0	0.0	0.0	11.2	489
12	61.4	27.6	0.0	0.0	10.2	438
13	55.4	38.2	0.0	0.0	6.4	582

with the teacher. This is basically a result of the class organization where pupils typically worked in groups of two on their science projects. Working together, they would often interact with the teacher together, although the boys, to a greater extent then the girls, would delegate communication with the teacher to one of the pair. The boys made a larger fraction of their moves when pupils were gathered as a total class than did the girls. In terms of the actual number of moves made in this context, however, boys and girls were more nearly equal.

Teacher and individual pupil. At the level of the individual pupil there is far more variety than the preceding tables would suggest. In both mathematics and science there were pupils who were never alone when they communicated with the teacher, others were always alone.[3] In social studies the range was from a student who was alone with the teacher for only 36 percent of his moves to one who was alone for all of them. Among those few pupils who made more than ten moves in each subject, one was alone with the teacher for 86 percent of her moves. Another was alone for only 29 percent of her moves. Most of the pupils

---

[3] When referring to behaviors of individual pupils, only those pupils are considered who made ten or more moves to the teacher in a particular subject area.

TABLE 2

Distribution of Moves by Boys and Girls in Groups of Different Sizes

		Percent of Moves Number of Pupils With the Teacher					f
Emitter	Subject	1	2	3	4	5+	
Boys							
	Mathematics	75.6	4.6	0.0	0.5	19.3	197
	Social Studies	77.4	8.1	2.2	1.6	10.7	372
	Science	50.7	39.9	0.0	0.8	8.6	353
Girls							
	Mathematics	88.5	4.2	0.2	0.0	7.1	521
	Social Studies	70.9	15.3	7.8	0.0	6.0	412
	Science	36.0	57.8	0.2	0.6	5.4	630

did not communicate with the teacher in a large group context. For some, however, large group interaction represented a substantial portion of their interactions, up to 36 percent in mathematics, 22 percent in social studies, and 23 percent in science.

Group Location

Teachers and pupils. Group size is one way of specifying the context of a move. A second type of context is the physical location of the group in which the move is made. It is evident from Table 3 that there is no fixed place for interactions between teacher and pupil. For each teacher there are sessions where the majority of moves are made at the desk (DKT) and sessions where the majority are made away from the desk. The moves made in the total classroom setting (CLR) vary from two percent to 32 percent of all moves made. It should be noted that class 9 is somewhat different in that all the pupils in that science class were involved in an experiment, which gave rise to more extensive teacher remarks to the class as a whole. The social studies classes began with class discussions of current events, which varied in duration, accounting for many of the CLR moves in classes 6, 7, and 8. Throughout, the variation seen within each subject area is more impressive than that seen between subjects.

Boys, girls, and teacher. Looking at the data by subject areas and in terms of where boys interact with the teacher as opposed to where

TABLE 3

Distribution of Moves in Various Locations for Individualized Classes

Class	UNC	CLR	DKT	DKP	MED	OTH	SEP	f
			Percent of Moves in Each Location					
1	0.0	7.6	35.7	22.1	26.3	1.9	5.8	807
2	0.0	16.5	54.2	19.5	0.0	3.3	6.6	570
3	0.0	25.1	0.0	66.0	0.0	1.0	7.8	398
6	0.0	16.6	30.6	28.0	7.6	10.0	7.2	500
7	0.0	16.9	29.5	25.7	3.5	12.8	11.6	509
8	0.0	2.4	80.2	3.5	0.0	3.3	10.6	659
9	0.0	32.0	2.4	60.5	0.0	2.4	2.7	532
10	0.0	9.5	2.7	67.0	0.0	14.7	6.1	441
11	0.0	11.0	84.0	0.0	0.0	0.0	4.9	489
12	0.0	11.0	49.7	6.2	14.8	7.3	21.2	438
13	0.0	6.0	87.0	0.0	0.0	3.3	3.7	582

girls do, the picture changes (Table 4). Boys tend to make a higher proportion of their moves in the total classroom context than do girls, although they are more nearly equal in terms of total number of moves. Girls tend to go to the teachers' desk more frequently than do boys and boys tend to have a higher proportion of their interactions with the teacher at their own desks. The rather higher MED figure for girls in mathematics represents extensive use of the blackboard by the teacher in working with a few girls. Amidst the diversity of figures, the consistency of those for moves made when the teacher and target pupil were separated is striking.

Teacher and individual pupil. Not surprisingly, the differences noted between boys and girls are nowhere as great as those between individual pupils. In every subject area there are boys and girls who make at least 65 percent more of their moves at the teachers' desks than do other boys and girls. Across all subjects, one pupil made 79 percent of his moves at the teacher's desk, another only sixteen percent. For moves made at the pupil's desk, the variation is almost as great. Across all classes one pupil made 68 percent of all his moves with the teacher at his own desk. Another made only four percent of his moves there. These figures suggest that some pupils are relatively passive in their interactions with the teacher, usually waiting for him to come to their desks. Other pupils are more active, regularly leaving their seats to interact with

TABLE 4

Distribution of Moves by Boys and Girls in Different Locations

Emitter	Subject	Percent of Moves in Each Location							f
		UNC	CLR	DKT	DKP	MED	OTH	SEP	
Boys									
	Mathematics	0.0	15.7	28.4	45.2	0.0	1.0	9.6	197
	Soc Studies	0.0	10.8	51.6	15.9	4.8	6.2	10.9	372
	Science	0.0	9.1	30.9	43.9	0.0	7.9	8.2	353
Girls									
	Mathematics	0.0	6.7	36.7	27.6	18.8	2.5	7.7	521
	Soc Studies	0.5	4.9	50.7	21.1	3.2	10.2	9.4	412
	Science	0.0	5.2	57.8	20.2	4.8	4.6	7.2	630

the teacher. These impressions of relative pupil activity are substantiated in the next chapter by our analysis of the types of moves made by the various classroom actors.

FOUR
The Data:
The Pedagogical Move

The pedagogical move is the basic unit used in the analysis of these classes. In this chapter we will look at the behaviors of the various classroom actors in terms of the amount of behavior, the type of behavior, and the form of behavior.

RELATIVE ACTIVITY OF CLASSROOM ACTORS

Teacher and pupils. Who makes the moves in this individualized game? As in Bellack's classes the teachers make the majority of moves in every class. The percentage of teacher moves ranges from 51 percent to 60 percent with a mean of 56 percent (Table 5). These are rather consistent figures. They fall well within the extremes of Bellack's classes, where the range was 33 percentage points, although the mean is seven percent lower than in his classes. The teacher, relative to students, was slightly less active in the individualized game, but still made 88 percent more moves than the teachers in Bellack's lecture-discussion classes. The number of teacher moves in the two sixth-grade lecture-discussion classes was even higher, however, which suggests that the age of the pupil participant has more to do with move frequencies than does instructional format. The increase in the number of moves is offset by the length of the move, which for both pupils and teachers was about one-third that in Bellack's classes.

Boys, girls, and teacher. The moves not made by the teacher are made by the pupils, but which ones? There is no reason to expect all pupils to participate equally and they do not. In this class of approximately equal numbers of boys and girls, the girls play a much more active game than do the boys. This is true for each subject and for all subjects together. The ratio of boys to girls varied from session to session as different pupils went to the library or into the field to work on a project. Sometimes a pupil was gone for a full period, sometimes for part

TABLE 5

Distribution of Moves by Various Emitters for Each Class

Class	Teacher	Percent by Each Emitter All Pupils*	Boy	Girl	A/V	f
1	57.0	42.8	4.9	36.4	0.1	807
2	60.5	39.4	14.3	23.1	0.0	570
3	56.0	43.7	18.8	23.8	0.2	398
4	59.1	40.8	16.1	19.5	0.0	822
5	58.7	41.0	14.3	23.8	0.1	730
6	51.4	48.6	20.4	26.8	0.0	500
7	52.0	47.7	19.8	26.5	0.1	509
8	51.5	48.4	25.6	21.6	0.0	659
9	54.6	45.3	19.3	20.8	0.0	532
10	60.0	39.9	21.9	15.1	0.0	441
11	55.8	44.1	8.9	30.8	0.0	489
12	56.6	43.3	10.0	30.8	0.0	438
13	56.7	43.2	11.1	28.5	0.0	582
INDIV	55.6	44.3	15.5	26.3	0.0	5925
4 + 5	58.9	40.9	15.3	21.5	0.0	1552

* Includes moves made by a group of pupils as well as an individual.

of a period. The overall ratio of girl minutes to boy minutes in the individualized classes was about 99:100. In the two lecture-discussion classes the amount of boy time and girl time in the class was equal. When the individual class figures are corrected for the actual amount of time boys and girls are in that class, it is only in class 10 that the average activity of a boy exceeds that of a girl. Across all classes, the average girl made 70 percent more moves than did the average boy. At least in this individualized sixth-grade class boys do not make as many moves as girls. For their part, the teacher made more moves directed toward girls than boys. The teacher-girl subgame is more common than the teacher-boy subgame.

Teacher and individual pupil. In terms of the teacher-pupil game, some of the pupils were sitting on the sidelines. On the typescripts made from the video-tapes, notation was made when pupils left and returned to the classroom. The number of moves made by a pupil and made by a teacher to that pupil were calculated per page of typescript for which the pupil was in the classroom. These figures were then adjusted to the common base of 100 pages of typescript. Teacher moves to a pupil per 100 pages of typescript for which that pupil was in the classroom varied from three to 147 in mathematics, from four to 86 in social studies, and from ten to 111 in science. Looking at the combined activity of all three teachers to a pupil, the range is not as great (thirteen to 80), which suggests that the same pupil did not receive the most moves from each teacher, nor the fewest. There were, however, pupils who consistently received more than their share of moves or fewer than their share of moves. Twenty-four percent of the pupils received above the median number of moves in each class. Twenty percent received fewer than the median number of moves in each of the three subjects. For moves made by the pupils the percentages are the same. Twenty-four percent made more than the median number of moves per 100 pages in each of the three subjects. Twenty percent made less. Since the distribution is highly skewed, it is informative to look at the means as well. Using the mean number of moves per 100 pages of typescript for a particular subject, no pupil made more than the average number of pupil moves in each of the three subject areas. Fifty-six percent of the pupils made fewer than the average number of moves in each of the three subjects. Eight percent of the pupils received more than the mean number of moves that a teacher made from each teacher. Thirty-six percent received fewer than the average number of moves from each teacher.

Analysis of the correlation of relative pupil activity in the three subjects shows the greatest relationship between mathematics and science ($r = .41$), next greatest between mathematics and social studies ($r = .15$), and the smallest correlation between social studies and science ($r = .05$). One can know almost nothing about how active a child will be in social studies by observing him in science. On the other hand, there is a significant relationship ($p < .05$) between a pupil's verbal activity with the science teacher and that with the mathematics teacher.

The ratio of a teacher's activity to that of his average pupil in terms of moves per class period ranged from 1.06:1 to 1.54:1. Again the variation is far greater on an individual basis. In mathematics the ratio ranged from 92:1 to 3.00:1. The range in social studies was .74:1 to 2.50:1 and in science it was 1.20:1 to 4.40:1. There were five pupils in social studies, one in mathematics, and none in science who made more moves than the teacher when interacting with him. Although there is considerable variation on an individual basis, the teacher almost always dominates the game.

Summary. This is only the roughest of overviews of the individualized game, but from it some interesting observations are possible. It should be clear that the variety of the individualized game is missed by a simple reporting of the relative number of moves made by the teacher and the collective pupil. The initial dichotomizing of pupils into boys and girls reveals the interesting fact that girls are almost three-fourths again as active with the teacher as boys. The further analysis of individual activity shows a situation where one pupil may be 49 times as active as another. What should be remembered in this, however, is that the teacher-pupil game is but a small part of the pupil's experience in the classroom and it may be that the pupil who is least involved with the teacher is the one who is best playing the individualized game. On the other hand it may be that those who are most active with the teacher are the ones who have best learned the rules of another game, the total class game, and who believe they will do best by properly courting the teacher.

It is time to turn from the mere fact of activity to the type of activity being performed. Do teachers and pupils perform the same functions in the individualized game, and do different pupils play the same sort of game with the teacher? The analysis of the various types of moves—structuring, soliciting, responding, and reacting—gives some answers to these questions.

MOVE FUNCTIONS: THE ROLES OF
TEACHERS AND PUPILS

Teacher and pupils. In the individualized classes teachers and pupils differ in the amount of their activity, although not so greatly as in Bellack's classes. They also differ in the type of activity they carry out, but again not so greatly as in Bellack's classes. The basic unit for analyzing classroom activity is the move. The move performs a pedagogical function. By comparing the extent to which different emitters use a given move, one determines the degree to which these emitters exercise a given function within the classroom. In Table 6 the relative teacher and pupil usage of each of the four pedagogical moves is presented both for Bellack's study and for the individualized and lecture-discussion classes of this study.

Most striking is the extent to which pupils structure in the individualized classes: they do so as often as the teacher. When a pupil approaches the teacher in the individualized class (and pupils initiate the teacher-pupil interaction 76 percent more often than does the teacher),[1]

[1] See Chapter 6 on interaction units.

TABLE 6

Pedagogical Roles of Teachers and Pupils

Move	Bellack's Study [a]			Individualized Class			Lecture-Discussion		
	f	% by T	% by P	f	% by T	% by P	f	% by T	% by P
STR	854	86.0	12.0	336	50.0	50.0	51	58.8	41.2
SOL	5135	86.0	14.0	2504	76.5	23.5	674	80.9	19.1
RES	4385	12.0	88.0	1607	18.5	81.5	432	3.9	96.1
REA	4649	81.0	19.0	1293	67.3	32.7	367	87.2	12.8

[a] Arno Bellack et al., The Language of the Classroom (New York: Teachers College Press, 1966), pp. 46, 47.

he often sets the context for what is to happen in that subgame by a structuring move. There are many such opportunities in the individualized game. In the classes observed pupils initiated interaction with the teacher 365 separate times.

Similarly impressive is the amount of reacting pupils do. In the lecture-discussion classes this is a function performed most of the time by the teacher, four times more frequently than by the pupil. In the individualized classes the teacher reacts only twice as often as the pupil. This is probably due to the basic nature of the individualized game where the pupil does more initiating (structuring and soliciting), the teacher as a result does more responding—over half again as much as in Bellack's classes—and the pupil has more opportunity for reacting. The relative use of the four moves by teachers and pupils in the lecture-discussion classes of this study tends to be more nearly that in Bellack's classes than for the individualized classes of this study. This suggests that the differences noted above are due to the instructional format rather than other factors.

The proportion of each move type made by the teacher and pupil was different from that found in Bellack's study. Each of these players also spent a different proportion of his time in the various functions than he did in the lecture-discussion classes (Table 7). Compared to Bellack's pupils, the ones in the individualized classes spent more time structuring by a factor of 3.7. They did 85 percent more soliciting, 23 percent less responding, and nine percent more reacting. In every instance there is a movement toward more equal use of each function. The teacher does 31 percent less structuring, 26 percent more soliciting, 64 percent more responding, and 32 percent less reacting than the teachers

TABLE 7

Distribution of Moves of Each Move Type for Each Class for Teacher and Pupil

Class	SRT	Percent by the Teacher SOL	RES	REA	f
1	2.8	59.7	8.6	27.3	460
2	4.0	56.5	8.1	31.3	345
3	6.7	64.1	7.6	20.6	223
4	2.2	62.1	1.2	34.3	486
5	4.4	56.6	2.5	35.6	429
6	6.2	54.8	10.1	28.4	257
7	6.0	54.7	11.3	27.1	265
8	3.5	58.5	12.6	24.1	340
9	8.5	67.0	2.4	20.9	291
10	4.5	56.2	10.9	27.1	265
11	8.0	54.2	11.3	24.9	273
12	3.6	56.4	7.6	27.8	248
13	5.1	56.9	8.7	28.4	330
INDIV	5.1	58.1	9.0	26.4	3297
4 + 5	3.2	59.5	1.8	34.9	915

in Bellack's study. Soliciting, which was the teachers' dominant behavior in the lecture-discussion classes, is even more prominent in the individualized classes. This soliciting is not the kind found in Bellack's classes. It contains a large number of directives. Over 40 percent of teacher solicitations prescribed, permitted, or prohibited pupil activity. The remaining solicitations that were not directives also were not part of the solicitation-response cycle which characterizes the traditional recitation. Almost three-fourths of the non-directive solicitations were void of reference to subject matter. Of all solicitations, only sixteen percent called for responses involving any subject matter. Solicitation remains the dominant function of the teacher, but it is a far different kind of solicitation from that of the traditional class.

Boys, girls, and teacher. One of the most striking results reported already was that girls were far more active than boys. The analysis of move types gives an equally striking result: girls play the game in a different way than boys. In terms of the moves girls made, a higher

STR	Percent by Pupils SOL	RES	REA	f
4.3	20.5	52.8	15.3	346
7.1	26.2	47.1	16.8	225
4.0	33.9	41.9	14.3	174
2.0	22.0	66.0	6.5	336
4.6	18.3	64.3	8.3	300
9.4	29.6	37.0	20.9	243
5.3	25.9	40.7	21.3	243
5.3	22.5	53.2	16.6	319
7.8	10.7	63.0	11.6	241
3.9	24.4	53.4	10.2	176
4.1	19.4	52.7	19.9	216
11.5	18.4	44.2	14.2	190
8.7	19.0	57.9	13.8	252
6.4	22.4	49.9	16.1	2625
3.3	20.2	65.2	7.3	636

proportion of them were structuring, soliciting, and reacting, a lower proportion were responding moves, than was the case with boys. After correcting for the amount of time actually spent in class by girls and by boys, the average girl made over twice as many initiatory moves (structuring and soliciting), twice as many reacting moves, and 45 percent more responding moves. Girls were more active participants than boys because they did far more initiating and they made the optional reacting move more frequently. It was the responding move that represented a greater proportion of the boys' moves than of the girls', and this move has an obligatory nature. It is called forth by a solicitation. The responder is expected to respond. The boys' activity was a forced activity a greater percentage of the time than was the girls'.

Although the girls were more active in the two lecture-discussion classes of this study, the pattern of their activity relative to boys' activity did not follow that of the individualized classes. In the lecture-discussion classes girls did 36 percent more initiating, 41 percent more responding, and 56 percent more reacting. Boys structured and solicited in a higher proportion of their moves than did girls.

Teacher and individual pupil. Role differences between individual pupils are usually greater than those between groups of pupils. Pupils act differently from one another in any given subject, and a given pupil may act in quite different ways from subject to subject. The ranges in percentage of time that individual pupils used a particular move vary greatly. Table 8 gives these ranges. To make these figures more concrete, in mathematics there was one pupil who did not make any initiatory move in the seventeen moves he made. Another, in twenty moves, was structuring or soliciting in twelve of them. In social studies, all sixteen of one pupil's moves were reflexive whereas another had fourteen of his twenty moves initiatory. In science the range was narrower with one pupil having as few as seventeen percent of his moves initiatory, another as many as 47 percent.

Some pupils do about the same amount of initiating from subject to subject. Other vary greatly, as much as from ten percent initiatory moves in mathematics to 70 percent in social studies. Figures such as these mean that the pupil is playing quite different roles in the two subject areas. In one she is passive, 90 percent of her moves being reflexive. In the other she is active, initiating further talk with the teacher in 70 percent of her moves. The individualized game allows for a great amount of variation, even within the same pupil.

Not surprisingly, differences in pupil behavior are related to teacher behaviors toward those pupils. If we correlate the number of initiatory moves (structuring and soliciting) made by a pupil with the total number of moves made by the teacher to that pupil, we find a strong relationship. The correlation coefficients for mathematics, science, and social studies are .86, .76, and .67 respectively, all significant beyond the .01 level. To a considerable extent, the pupil who did not direct structuring or soliciting moves to the teacher did not get the teacher's attention.

With pupils playing different roles in the individualized game, the teacher's role changed depending on the pupil's interaction with him. Table 9 presents the range of teacher use of the different moves with pupils to whom he directed ten or more moves.

In mathematics and social studies over 80 percent of the teachers' moves to some pupils were initiatory, to others less than half of the teachers' moves were initiatory. In science a range of from 52 percent to 92 percent of all teacher moves to individual pupils were initiatory. Individual pupils experienced a range of teacher behaviors across the three subjects, a range as great as from 44 percent to 72 percent initia-

TABLE 8
Range of Individual Pupil Use of Each Move Type in Each Subject

Move	Mathematics	Social Studies	Science
STR	0.0%–18.2%	0.0%–11.1%	0.0%–35.3%
SOL	0.0%–48.3%	0.0%–60.0%	10.1%–41.9%
RES	9.1%–70.6%	10.0%–60.0%	28.6%–73.3%
REA	5.0%–40.0%	0.0%–29.0%	0.0%–34.2%

TABLE 9
Range of Teacher Use of Each Move Type Across Individual Pupils

Move	Mathematics	Social Studies	Science
STR	0.0%–13.3%	0.0%–14.3%	0.0%– 9.1%
SOL	45.0%–75.0%	32.4%–75.9%	49.1%–83.3%
RES	0.0%–13.3%	0.0%–25.0%	3.6%–18.2%
REA	20.0%–46.7%	5.9%–41.7%	0.0%–37.0%

tory moves and as small as from 60 percent to 65 percent initiatory moves. These are fairly large differences in teacher role, although not nearly so great as the differences in roles played by pupils.

Summary. We have looked at the functions of teachers and pupils at progressively individual levels. The emerging picture is one in which the roles of teacher and pupil are less rule governed than would be expected from looking at the class figures. Even at the individual level, however, the predominant teacher function was nearly always soliciting. This held true in 62 of the 63 teacher-pupil groupings where the teacher made ten or more moves. Although not quite so overwhelmingly, the pupil function of responding usually predominated. This was true of 44 of the 55 pupil-teacher combinations in which pupils made ten or more moves. Even with all the individual variety there is some consistency.

THE FORM OF THE MOVE

Teacher and pupils. The pedagogical move is a functional move and as such is not limited to speaking. Soliciting, for example, may be done through speaking, gesturing, writing, uttering some sound such as "hmmmmm?", or through some combination of these forms. At least for the classes of this study, the form of the move appears to be dependent on the type of game being played (individualized or lecture-discussion) and on the player's position in the game (teacher or pupil). As may be seen in Table 10, the form also varies with the type of move.

Within the individualized classes only three percent of all teacher moves involve no speaking (i.e., WRI plus GES). In these same classes twelve percent of the pupils' initiatory moves and seventeen percent of their reflexive moves were emitted with no speaking. These included raising the hand to indicate a need for help, pointing out an answer, and so forth. Pupils also conveyed the meaning of an initiatory move through a combination of speaking and gesturing (SPK/GES) more frequently than did teachers. A common example of this move form was: "Hey Mr. Mandel, sign this for me." In some cases the teacher response to this sort of move was simply to write (WRI).

In the two lecture-discussion classes there was a marked increase in pupil initiatory moves whose form was gesturing (GES) and in teacher reflexive moves whose form was speaking and writing (SPK/WRI). To a large extent the interaction between teacher and pupil in the lecture-discussion class was initiated by the pupil's raising his hand, indicating that he wanted to speak. The large number of pupil initiatory moves whose form was gesturing is the primary explanation for the decrease in percentage of moves whose form was speaking as well as speaking and gesturing. The increase in teacher moves whose form was speaking and writing may well be an anomaly of the two periods when the lecture-discussion method was used. In these classes the teacher was solving problems at the chalk board under the direction of the class. There were many reactions where the teacher wrote what the pupil said and himself said something in addition to the writing. Overall, it appears that the pupil relies more on the gesture to convey part or all of his meaning than does the teacher, and that he does so more with initiatory moves in the lecture-discussion classes and more with reflexive moves in the individualized classes.

Boys, girls, and teacher. In the preceding section move form was seen to vary with the emitter, the move, and the instructional format. Move form also appears to vary, although to a lesser extent, with the

TABLE 10

Move Form, Emitter, and Move Type

Emitter and Move	Percent of Moves in Each Form						*f*
	SKP	SND	WRI	GES	SPK/ WRI	SPK/ GES	
Individualized							
T STR and SOL	87.3	0.0	0.1	1.7	1.8	9.1	2084
T RES and REA	85.0	0.4	2.5	1.6	3.8	6.7	1167
P STR and SOL	65.7	0.0	0.0	12.5	0.1	21.7	756
P RES and REA	77.7	0.4	0.5	16.6	0.3	4.5	1733
Lecture-Discussion							
T STR and SOL	82.1	0.0	0.0	4.7	5.6	7.6	575
T RES and REA	71.2	0.0	1.2	0.6	24.6	2.4	337
P STR and SOL	34.6	0.7	0.0	60.0	0.7	4.0	150
P RES and REA	85.9	0.2	1.1	9.7	1.1	2.0	462

gender of the pupil emitter. In each subject area, boys used gestures to communicate their meaning a greater proportion of the time than did girls. Boys gestured in at least 50 percent more of their moves than did girls in each subject area. For this class, girls' moves have a verbal component a higher proportion of the time than do boys', and boys' moves have a non-verbal component a higher proportion of the time than do girls'.

Teacher and individual pupil. At the level of the individual pupil, there was no pupil who made ten or more moves in a subject who did not rely on gesturing to convey at least part of the meaning. One pupil used gesturing in as few as five percent of his moves, another in as many as 47 percent. This is not to say that gesturing of one sort or another did not accompany other moves, but that often gestures were essential to the communication of meaning. Gestures which were redundant in terms of the cognitive meaning or which expressed an emotional meaning were not coded.

SUMMARY

We have been looking at one aspect of individualized instruction, teacher-pupil interaction. For some pupils this accounts for a significant portion of classroom time. For others, interaction with the teacher is almost non-existent. The most extreme example was in mathematics where one pupil made 49 times more moves than did another. Pupils differed in the type of activity as well as the amount. In a given class, some pupils make mostly initiatory moves, others only reflexive moves. A given pupil may make mostly initiatory moves in one class, mostly reflexive moves in another. Individualization allows for large variations in pupil classroom roles. The teacher's role tends to vary in a complementary fashion to that of the pupil with whom he is interacting. In the individualized setting we have also seen wide variation in ways pupils express themselves. Some rely on gestures in nearly half their moves, others in very few. At the individual level, the analysis shows great variety.

By grouping boys and girls we see a number of interesting things. Girls are much more active with the teacher, 70 percent more so than the average boy. They are active in different ways. A higher proportion of their moves are structuring and soliciting, in which the emitter takes the initiative, and reacting, which is an optional move. When a boy makes a move it is more likely to be a responding move than it is when a girl makes the move. Responding moves are called for by teachers' soliciting moves. Girls are more active, their activity is characterized by a higher proportion of moves freely made, and their activity more verbal than that of boys. Boys rely much more on gestures in the communication of meaning.

At the most general level, that of teachers and pupils, we have seen familiar results. The teacher is consistently more active than the pupils. He makes more moves, although not to so great an extent as has been observed in other contexts. The teacher is primarily a solicitor. He makes more solicitations than all other moves combined. Relatively, however, he does not dominate the soliciting function as thoroughly as do teachers in other contexts. In these individualized classes pupils made nearly one-fourth of all soliciting moves. In general, the teachers and pupils in these individualized classes used each move to a more nearly equal extent than has been found in other types of classes.

The question must finally come: what are they talking about in all these moves? In the next chapter we answer this question.

FIVE

The Data: Meanings Expressed Through the Move

THE SUBSTANTIVE/INSTRUCTIONAL DICHOTOMY

Teacher and pupils. In individualized classes the predominance of teacher solicitations and pupil responses was not related to traditional recitation with a subject-matter focus. The reason for this should be clear from Table 11. Although solicitations and responses predominate, substantive meanings do not.

Only sixteen percent of all moves in the individualized classes had substantive meanings. Within each subject there was considerable variation from period to period, yet in none did the proportion of moves having substantive meaning reach 30 percent of all moves. This contrasts sharply with Bellack's study, where no class spent less than half its time with subject matter and some classes communicated subject matter in over 80 percent of all moves. The relative proportion of substantive and instructional moves in the two lecture-discussion classes of this study was closer to that of Bellack's classes than the individualized classes.

The data reported here are not fully comparable to Bellack's because of the coding of non-verbal moves. A pupil raising his hand and the teacher pointing to him to talk would both be coded as non-verbal instructional moves in this study and would not have been coded in Bellack's study. Thus our percentages of substantive meanings would have been somewhat higher had non-verbal moves not been coded. As noted in the previous chapter, this type of non-verbal initiation by pupils and response by teachers was not nearly so common in the individualized classes as in the lecture discussion classes. As a result the percentage of substantive moves in the individualized classes can more accurately be compared to Bellack's figures.

Given these considerations, the lecture-discussion classes of this study are even closer to Bellack's classes, in terms of proportion of substantive moves, than they appear to be from the figures. It seems highly

TABLE 11

Substantive and Instructional Meanings for Each Class

Class	Substantive Moves			Instructional Moves			All Moves *	
	% by T	% by P	f	% by T	% by P	f	% Substantive	% Instructional
1	55.0	45.0	200	60.8	39.1	600	25.6	76.9
2	54.5	45.4	88	62.1	37.8	484	15.7	86.4
3	42.8	57.1	70	60.6	39.3	323	18.0	83.4
6	54.5	45.4	121	51.9	48.0	387	24.5	78.6
7	50.6	49.3	81	54.5	45.4	425	16.5	86.7
8	46.6	53.3	30	52.1	47.8	621	4.6	95.8
9	46.0	53.9	152	60.6	39.3	366	29.6	71.3
10	55.1	44.8	49	62.8	37.1	377	11.5	88.9
11	52.6	47.3	38	56.7	43.2	444	7.9	93.0
12	59.0	40.9	22	58.5	41.4	386	5.4	95.3
13	45.9	54.0	61	57.8	42.1	522	10.5	90.1
INDIV	51.2	48.7	912	57.9	42.0	4935	15.8	85.7
4 + 5	50.5	49.4	686	69.1	30.8	923	44.9	60.4

* The percentage of substantive and instructional moves may sum to more than 100% because some moves had both substantive and instructional meaning.

likely that the differences between the individualized and lecture-discussion classes are due to the type of game being played rather than to factors of age or subject matter.

Boys, girls, and teacher. At a finer level of analysis, girls communicate subject matter more frequently than do boys. Twenty percent of girls' moves have substantive meanings as compared to fifteen percent of boys' moves. The picture is not consistent across subject areas, however. In mathematics twelve percent of boys' moves have substantive meanings as compared to 29 percent of girls' moves. In social studies the figures are twelve percent and fifteen percent, whereas in science there is a reversal, with boys communicating subject matter in nineteen percent of their moves compared to sixteen percent for girls.

Teacher and individual pupil. As expected, the variation between players is much greater on the individual level. The ranges for percent of moves conveying subject matter, for pupils with ten or move moves, are as follows: mathematics zero to 62 percent; social studies zero to 54 percent; and science zero to 35 percent. The percent of substantive moves made by a given player varies across subject areas by as much as 34 percentage points. For some the game with the teacher is one of talking about assignments, materials, leaving the room, and so forth. For others there is a significant subject matter component.

The teacher's part in the individualized game is complementary to the pupil's. Each teacher fails to communicate subject matter with some pupils. With others, as many as 55 percent of the mathematics teacher's moves, 54 percent of the social studies teacher's moves, and 27 percent of the science teacher's moves contain substantive meanings. Not surprisingly, those pupils who communicate the most subject matter to the teacher are those to whom the teacher directs the greatest amount of subject matter. Over all classes, the correlation between the number of substantive moves made by a pupil and the number of substantive moves made by teachers to that pupil is a highly significant (beyond .01) .96.

SUBSTANTIVE MEANINGS

Bellack analyzed substantive meanings through categories which basically represented an outline of the pamphlet on which the classes were based. There was no such option in this study. Instead, substantive meanings were coded according to whether they were relevant to the subject area. Across all individualized classes, only one percent of the substantive moves were coded as not relevant to the subject area. This is not greatly different from Bellack's figure of four percent of the substantive moves being on something other than trade. Overall the pupils made a higher proportion of non-relevant moves than the teachers. Among the pupils the girls did so more frequently than the boys. The range is small, however, from one percent of teachers' moves being non-relevant to two percent for girls. These trends were not consistent across all subject areas.

SUBSTANTIVE LOGICAL MEANINGS

Teacher and pupils. When considered at the more general level, the proportions of the various logical processes used to convey substantive meanings are remarkably similar to the figures reported by Bellack. Twelve percent of Bellack's substantive moves were coded in the analytic process categories of defining or interpreting. The corresponding figure for the individualized classes is also twelve percent. Bellack coded 81 percent of the moves in the empirical process categories of stating or explaining fact. Eighty-four percent of the substantive moves in this study were so coded. The evaluative process categories of opining and justifying were coded for seven percent of Bellack's substantive moves and for four percent in this study.

Looking within the categories and within subject areas, the similarities are not so strong as when the categories are collapsed into the empirical, analytical, and evaluative processes. In the individualized mathematics classes of this study interpreting was done four times more frequently than in the other classes or than in Bellack's classes. In the individualized mathematics and social studies classes fact stating is used far more frequently (by a factor of 2.8) than explaining, whereas in the science class the figures of 40 percent fact stating and 49 percent explaining are much closer to Bellack's figures of 35 percent and 46 percent. Finally, in the individualized mathematics and science classes the processes of opining and justifying were rarely used. The figures for social studies of eight percent opining and one percent justifying are similar to those found for Bellack's classes, which were also in social studies. Generally, the simpler logical processes of defining, interpreting, fact stating, and opining are used a higher percent of the time with the sixth graders of this study and the more complex logical processes of explaining and justifying are more used in the high school classes of Bellack's study.

Boys, girls, and teacher. When teachers, boys, and girls are considered separately, there is a remarkable consistancy in the relative frequencies with which they use each of the substantive logical categories. Table 12 presents these figures. Differences in the ways these players

TABLE 12

Use of Each Substantive Logical Process by Teacher, Boys, and Girls

Emitter	Percent of Moves in Each Category						
	DEF	INT	FAC	XPL	OPN	JUS	*f*
Teacher	6.6	3.9	53.1	32.8	3.2	0.4	467
Boys	9.4	2.3	53.9	27.3	7.0	0.0	128
Girls	7.9	4.9	54.9	29.9	2.3	0.0	304
Pupils	8.3	4.3	53.5	30.1	3.8	0.0	445

play the game are not reflected in their use of logical processes. Analysis of individual pupil activity is not possible because of the low frequencies with which any of them make moves with substantive meanings.

INSTRUCTIONAL MEANINGS

We have seen that the talk between teachers and pupils in these individualized classes seldom deals with subject matter. Instructional meanings are the meanings most frequently communicated. As we examine these meanings we will deviate from our practice of looking from the general to the specific. The reason for this is the considerable uniformity in use of the instructional meaning categories. Correlating the use of these categories by all emitters in each of the three subjects, the similarity is striking. Coefficients of .93, .97, and .97 were obtained when comparing the patterns of usage in math and science, math and social studies, and social studies and science, respectively. Overall, teachers and pupils as well as boys and girls behave in highly similar fashions. The correlations in their use of the various instructional meaning categories are .95 and .99, respectively. Cursory inspection of the data in Table 13 reveals the similar patterns of usage leading to these high correlations.

It may be difficult to imagine the kind of interchanges that avoid subject matter. The following sequence is fairly representative of types of moves made in these classes:

P. Should I do another "information" for extra credit, even
if I don't have all this work done?   ASG
T. Why don't you do number three? That deals with

TABLE 13

Distribution of Instructional Moves in Instructional Meaning Categories

Class	Emitter	Percent of Moves in Each Category			
		PRC	MAT	STA	ASG
Individualized					
Mathematics	All	6.1	8.8	13.8	38.8
	Teacher	6.9	9.2	18.6	39.5
	Pupil(s)	4.8	8.3	6.2	37.8
	Boy	6.5	12.3	4.5	28.4
	Girl	3.9	7.0	7.0	40.7
Social Studies	All	6.1	12.9	14.4	35.2
	Teacher	6.2	12.4	17.0	36.3
	Pupil(s)	6.5	13.5	11.4	33.9
	Boy	5.0	11.0	11.3	36.8
	Girl	7.0	16.1	11.4	32.0
Science	All	12.5	15.8	14.0	35.7
	Teacher	12.1	14.5	18.3	35.5
	Pupil(s)	13.1	17.5	7.7	36.1
	Boy	13.3	10.9	7.4	38.3
	Girl	14.0	20.1	8.7	36.0
All Classes	All	8.8	13.0	14.1	36.5
	Teacher	9.0	12.3	18.0	36.8
	Pupil(s)	8.7	13.9	8.6	36.1
	Boy	8.3	11.3	8.6	35.8
	Girl	9.1	15.2	9.0	36.4
Lecture Discussion					
Mathematics	All	3.8	3.4	31.4	6.4
	Teacher	3.8	2.4	42.6	6.3
	Pupil(s)	3.9	5.6	6.3	6.7
	Boy	5.3	4.2	2.1	6.3
	Girls	3.0	7.1	7.1	5.3

		Percent of Moves in Each Category						
PER	LOG	ACT	ACV	ACP	ACC	ACE	LAM	f
2.6	0.1	1.5	10.2	2.4	14.0	0.9	0.1	1407
2.6	0.1	1.4	8.6	8.6	10.2	1.2	0.1	862
2.8	0.0	1.6	12.7	3.7	19.8	0.6	0.2	545
5.8	0.0	1.3	16.8	4.5	17.4	0.0	0.0	168
1.1	0.0	1.7	11.8	2.0	23.0	1.4	0.3	356
4.2	0.1	3.6	6.9	5.9	9.5	0.3	1.0	1433
4.2	0.1	2.5	7.1	4.8	8.9	0.3	0.8	757
4.1	0.1	4.9	6.7	7.3	10.1	0.3	1.2	676
2.5	0.3	6.3	6.6	6.9	11.6	0.6	0.6	319
5.9	0.0	3.8	7.0	5.3	9.1	0.0	1.8	341
0.6	0.1	1.2	5.3	4.7	8.1	1.3	0.5	2095
0.5	0.2	1.1	4.4	3.6	7.7	1.9	0.2	1239
0.7	0.0	1.3	6.5	6.4	8.8	0.5	0.9	856
0.8	0.0	1.2	9.4	3.5	13.7	0.8	0.4	267
0.4	0.0	1.4	5.7	4.5	6.9	0.4	1.4	507
2.2	0.1	2.0	7.2	4.4	10.2	0.9	0.5	4935
2.1	0.1	1.6	6.4	3.3	8.7	1.2	0.4	2858
2.4	0.0	2.6	8.2	6.0	12.2	0.6	0.8	2077
2.6	0.1	3.5	9.8	5.5	13.7	0.5	0.4	754
2.2	0.0	2.2	7.9	4.0	12.3	0.6	1.2	1204
2.5	0.2	2.5	25.6	5.4	18.9	0.0	0.0	923
2.0	0.3	2.7	19.1	4.5	16.3	0.0	0.0	638
3.5	0.0	2.1	40.0	7.4	24.6	0.0	0.0	285
4.2	0.0	2.1	50.5	5.3	20.0	0.0	0.0	95
2.4	0.0	1.8	39.1	5.3	29.0	0.0	0.0	169

modern Italy. I think you might be interested in knowing
something about that.   ASG
P. O.K. (pause).   STA
But I haven't finished my other report.   ASG
T. Oh.   ACC
P. We don't have any of the other books though.   MAT
T. Oh.   ACC

Assignment (ASG). This part of the conversation focuses primarily
on what the pupil is to do (ASG), with lesser emphasis on materials,
statements, or cognitive actions. Indeed, over one-third of all instructional moves focus primarily on assignments (see Table 13). Moreover, there is remarkably little variation between teachers and pupils
or across subject areas. This individualized format seems to require that
teacher and pupil spend much of their time talking about what work a
pupil has completed, what he is to do next, evaluation of this work, and
the rate at which the pupil is working.

In the initial analysis of these classrooms the ASG category was
subdivided to differentiate between general talk about assignments,
evaluations of pupil work, and comments about the progress a pupil
had or had not made. Although there is similarity in the overall ASG
figures, differences emerge in the subcategories of evaluation and pupil
progress. In mathematics 44 percent of the moves coded ASG dealt with
evaluation, eighteen percent with pupil progress. The corresponding
figures for social studies were twelve percent and 46 percent. In science
they were one percent and 40 percent. The different amounts of talk
about evaluation of a pupil's work and his rate of progress in his work
were directly related to what was happening in the classes. In mathematics, tests were taken after given portions of the text had been completed. In fact, progress was shown by the number of tests taken. It was
also easy for this teacher to ascertain pupil progress simply by walking
around the room and checking which page a pupil was on. In science
the teacher only needed to know which step of the project a pupil was on
since all steps had to be taken in order. In social studies there were film
strips to be watched and summarized, reports to be written, and work-
sheets to be completed. Since these were done in different sequences, the
teacher had to determine where the pupil was in each type of activity.

Statement (STA). A move is coded STA when its primary reference
is to a previous statement. Fourteen percent of all instructional moves
refer to preceding moves. STA is most frequently coded when one

speaker is showing acceptance, approval, or disapproval of what another has said. The rating of another's utterance is more common to the teacher role than to the pupil role in most school contexts. These individualized classes are no exception. Thus the similarity between teachers and pupils which exists in their use of most instructional meaning categories is absent here. STA is coded much less frequently in individualized classes than in lecture-discussion classes. In our classes the object of a teacher rating is frequently the work a pupil has actually done (ASG) rather than what he has said (STA). Ratings in lecture-discussion classes are almost always of what a pupil has said.

Material (MAT). The third most frequently expressed instructional meaning is related to materials. As with the ASG category, the MAT category was initially subdivided for this study. It was felt that materials became far more important when instruction was individualized. Thus, a range of categories was needed to specify in more detail the range of materials used. Accordingly, five subcategories were created: books, magazines, and reproduced materials; audiovisual hardware and software; instructional apparatus; supplies; and noninstructional materials. Surprisingly, only thirteen percent of the moves referred to materials. Supplies were referred to most frequently, in less than four percent of the instructional moves. Pupil activity with materials dominated these classes, yet materials were not often the focus of teacher-pupil conversations.

Across subject areas there is greater variation in the degree to which materials were coded than for most of the instructional meaning categories. This variation parallels the amount of freedom pupils had in what they did. In mathematics all pupils had the same texts and supplies. In science different materials, often not immediately available, were needed for each pair of pupils. With greater diversity in the materials used came a greater need to talk about them.

Procedure (PRC). The procedure category was also coded most frequently in science, and again the reason is clear. The steps in the science projects were sequential, and the sequence was new to the pupils. They repeatedly needed information on how to procede. In social studies activities were shorter, there was no necessary sequence to them, and they usually involved skills which the pupils already possessed. There was very little talk about how to use the library or summarize filmstrips. In mathematics, too, the procedures were well known.

Activities (ACT, ACV, ACP, ACC and ACE). Nearly one-fourth of the instructional moves referred to activities of various sorts, most frequently to cognitive activity (ACC). "You got that?" and "All clear now?" and "O.K.?" are among the various parting comments a teacher makes as a final check to make sure a pupil knows what to do, where mistakes are, and so on. A student statement such as "I don't know" or "I don't understand" is often the entry point for a pupil's talk with a teacher. Moves which refer primarily to one's cognitive state are coded ACC. Pupils tend to make these moves more frequently than teachers.

Another fairly frequently coded activity category has vocal activity (ACV) as its referant. These moves may be directives to speak louder or to repeat what has been said. They may also be comments on the way one talks or requests for permission to speak. Moves coded ACV are much less frequent in individualized classes, probably because there is not the same need to control the amount and kind of vocal participation as there is in lecture-discussion classes. The other activity categories are used somewhat less often than ACC or ACV.

Other categories. As in Bellack's senior high classes, only a fraction of a percent of the instructional moves were devoted to the logic of the material (LOG) or to language mechanics (LAM). Comments about one's person (PER)—such as "What kind of pin is that?"—were somewhat more common in the individualized classes. There is certainly more opportunity for this type of comment when talking with only one or two pupils.

It has already been noted that the coding of the different instructional meaning categories was very similar from one individualized class to the next. There is also a similarity between the coding of instructional meanings for the lecture-discussion classes of this study and of Bellack's study. The correlation coefficient is a significant .87. When the individualized classes are compared to the lecture-discussion classes, however, these correlations drop to .26. The type of instructional meanings communicated appear to vary with instructional format rather than teacher, subject area, or age of pupils.

INSTRUCTIONAL LOGICAL MEANINGS:
LOGICAL CATEGORIES

Each move with instructional meaning has an associated instructional logical meaning. These meanings are of two types. The logical meaning categories are the same as those through which substantive meanings are analyzed, with rating categories added. The second type of meaning is extra-logical. Extra-logical categories are used in conjunction with directives, that is, utterances which prescribe, permit, or prohibit activity.

Teacher and pupils. In the individualized classes 68 percent of the instructional moves were expressed through logical processes as opposed to extra-logical processes. In Bellack's study 77 percent of the instructional moves involved logical processes. In that study fact stating (FAC) accounted for 26 percent of the instructional moves and rating statements for 44 percent. The remaining seven percent were divided between the explaining (XPL), defining (DEF), opining (OPN), justifying (JUS), and interpreting (INT) categories.[1] In the individualized classes nearly twice as many moves are accounted for by explaining and fact stating while considerably fewer, only thirteen percent of the instructional moves, are ratings (Table 14). This is basically a reflection of the differences between the individualized format and the more traditional subject-matter-dominated recitation format where the teacher regularly rates the pupils' substantive responses. Although the percentage of ratings in this study is far smaller, the overall ratio of positive (POS) to negative (NEG and QAL), 4.2:1, is not greatly different from the 3.2:1 figure in Bellack's study. It is particularly interesting that upon separate analysis of teacher and pupil ratings, we find these teachers rate pupils positively in the ratio of 4.8:1 whereas the pupil's rating of the teachers is in the ratio of 2.3 positive ratings for each negative rating. Pupils rate teachers far less frequently than teachers rate pupils, but when they do they are more than twice as likely to give a negative or qualifying rating.

In the lecture-discussion classes of this study, the various instructional logical categories were used in proportions closer to those found by Bellack than to those for the individualized classes of this study. Thus the instructional logical differences between these individualized classes and Bellack's are probably due more to differences in instructional mode than to grade level or teacher factors.

Boys, girls, and teacher. Looking at the proportions in which boys' and girls' moves were coded in the various instructional logical categories, one is impressed by the similarity in the way they play the individualized game. The only striking dissimilarity is in the teachers' behavior, specifically their relative use of positive and negative ratings with boys and girls. Girls' ratings were more likely to be positive than were boys'. This was true across each class and across all classes combined. Across all classes the ratio of positive to negative ratings for boys was 3.5:1. For girls the figure was 5.9:1 (Table 15).

[1] Arno Bellack *et al., The Language of the Classroom* (New York: Teachers College Press, 1966), pp. 80, 81.

TABLE 14

Distribution of Moves in Each Instructional Logical Category

Class	Emitter	DEF	INT	FAC	XPL	OPN	JUS	NCL	POS	NEG
				Percent of Moves in Each Category						
Individualized										
Mathematics	Teacher	0.0	1.0	40.1	3.0	2.4	0.1	0.6	16.0	2.4
	Pupil(s)	0.0	2.0	55.4	2.7	2.2	0.1	0.7	2.9	1.2
	Boy	0.0	1.7	55.3	4.1	2.3	0.5	0.0	2.3	1.1
	Girl	0.0	2.2	55.8	2.2	2.2	0.0	0.5	3.3	0.8
	All	0.0	1.4	46.0	2.9	2.3	0.1	0.7	10.9	1.9
Social Studies	Teacher	0.0	1.7	44.9	5.0	3.8	0.3	0.0	10.8	3.8
	Pupil(s)	0.0	1.9	54.2	5.0	2.5	0.0	0.4	4.2	2.2
	Boy	0.0	1.8	52.6	5.9	2.5	0.0	0.6	5.3	1.8
	Girl	0.0	2.0	56.5	4.3	2.6	0.0	0.2	3.5	2.0
	All	0.0	1.8	49.3	5.0	3.2	0.2	0.2	7.7	3.0
Science	Teacher	0.1	1.0	38.8	4.4	1.2	0.0	0.3	17.0	0.6
	Pupil(s)	0.2	1.8	50.5	7.2	1.4	0.0	0.1	3.1	0.9
	Boy	0.0	1.8	47.5	9.3	1.1	0.0	0.0	3.3	1.4
	Girl	0.3	2.1	52.0	7.1	1.7	0.0	0.0	3.1	0.7
	All	0.1	1.3	43.6	5.5	1.3	0.0	0.2	11.3	0.7
All Classes	Teacher	0.0	1.2	40.8	4.1	2.3	0.1	0.3	15.0	2.0
	Pupil(s)	0.0	1.9	53.0	5.3	1.9	0.0	0.3	3.4	1.4
	Boy	0.0	1.8	51.4	6.7	1.9	0.1	0.2	3.9	1.5
	Girl	0.1	2.1	54.4	4.9	2.1	0.0	0.2	3.3	1.1
	All	0.0	1.5	45.9	4.6	2.1	0.1	0.3	10.1	1.7
Lecture-Discussion										
Mathematics	Teacher	0.0	0.3	26.4	1.0	2.1	0.0	0.0	34.3	5.3
	Pupil(s)	0.0	0.0	36.8	1.7	2.8	0.0	0.3	4.2	3.1
	Boy	0.0	0.0	34.7	1.0	4.2	0.0	0.0	1.0	3.1
	Girl	0.0	0.0	41.4	2.3	0.0	0.0	0.0	4.1	2.9
	All	0.0	0.2	29.6	1.3	2.3	0.0	0.1	25.0	4.6

Teacher and individual pupil. If we look again at those pupils in each subject who received ten or more moves from the teacher, we see that almost all received some positive ratings (Table 16). In mathematics no such pupil failed to receive a positive rating. In social studies and science there were two and one such pupils respectively. Almost all pupils received positive ratings each week in each of the three individualized classes. Negative ratings were also common. Between 55 percent and 58 percent of the pupils in each subject who were targets for ten or more teacher moves received negative or qualifying ratings.

					Percent of Moves in Each Category						
PON	QAL	PRE	PER	PRO	PTR	DIR	RPR	COM	ALT	NCM	ƒ
0.0	1.7	18.3	8.7	1.3	2.5	0.3	0.1	0.9	0.0	0.0	862
2.5	0.0	1.1	0.0	0.0	0.1	4.0	10.2	14.1	0.1	0.0	545
2.3	0.0	1.7	0.0	0.0	0.5	1.7	11.9	13.6	0.0	0.0	168
2.8	0.0	0.8	0.0	0.0	0.0	5.3	9.8	13.4	0.2	0.0	356
0.9	1.0	11.6	5.3	0.8	1.6	1.7	4.0	6.0	0.0	0.0	1407
0.2	1.0	15.5	7.3	1.9	1.7	0.1	0.0	1.1	0.1	0.0	757
0.0	0.4	2.0	0.0	0.2	0.8	3.4	7.9	13.9	0.1	0.1	676
0.0	0.3	1.8	0.0	0.0	0.9	3.4	7.8	14.7	0.0	0.0	319
0.0	0.5	2.3	0.0	0.5	0.8	3.2	8.5	11.7	0.2	0.2	341
0.1	0.7	9.2	3.9	1.1	1.3	1.6	3.7	7.1	0.1	0.0	1433
0.3	0.8	21.2	5.0	0.9	2.0	0.0	0.3	5.3	0.0	0.0	1239
0.0	0.0	6.3	0.4	0.1	0.3	2.9	4.9	18.4	0.8	0.1	856
0.0	0.0	7.8	0.3	0.0	0.0	1.1	7.8	17.6	0.3	0.0	267
0.0	0.0	6.5	0.5	0.1	0.5	4.3	4.1	14.7	1.1	0.1	507
0.1	0.4	15.1	3.1	0.6	1.3	1.1	2.1	10.6	0.3	0.0	2095
0.2	1.1	18.8	6.7	1.3	2.1	0.1	0.1	2.9	0.0	0.0	2858
0.6	0.1	3.5	0.1	0.1	0.4	3.3	7.3	15.8	0.4	0.0	2077
0.5	0.1	3.9	0.1	0.0	0.5	2.2	8.7	15.5	0.1	0.0	754
0.8	0.1	3.6	0.2	0.2	0.4	4.3	7.0	13.5	0.6	0.1	1204
0.4	0.7	12.4	4.0	0.8	1.4	1.4	3.1	8.3	0.2	0.0	4935
2.0	1.4	7.6	15.0	0.9	2.3	0.4	0.0	0.3	0.0	0.0	638
0.3	0.0	1.0	0.0	0.0	0.3	2.1	33.3	13.6	0.0	0.0	285
0.0	0.0	1.0	0.0	0.0	1.0	1.0	44.2	8.4	0.0	0.0	95
0.5	0.0	0.5	0.0	0.0	0.0	2.9	31.3	13.6	0.0	0.0	169
1.5	0.9	5.6	10.4	0.6	1.7	0.9	10.2	4.4	0.0	0.0	923

INSTRUCTIONAL LOGICAL MEANINGS: EXTRA-LOGICAL CATEGORIES

Requests for directives (DIR) and requests for permission (RPR), directives which prescribe (PRE), permit (PER), or prohibit (PRO) an activity, and responses to a directive such as compliance (COM), giving an alternative (ALT), and noncompliance (NCM) are considered to have extra-logical meaning. From the data in Table 14 it is evident that use of these categories varies greatly from teacher to pupil; boys and girls use a category of behavior to about the same extent.

TABLE 15

Distribution of Teacher Instructional Moves Directed to Specific Targets and Using Selected Logical Processes

Class	Target	FAC	XPL	POS	NEG	PRE	PER	PRO	f
					Percent of Moves in Each Category				
Individualized									
Mathematics	Class	54.8	6.7	3.8	1.9	25.0	0.0	7.7	104
	Boys	38.0	2.8	13.2	5.6	19.2	8.8	0.8	248
	Girls	37.5	2.6	20.2	4.0	15.2	10.5	0.4	505
Social Studies	Class	36.8	2.6	7.8	7.8	31.5	2.6	5.2	37
	Boys	46.7	5.3	9.9	5.1	16.5	6.9	2.6	365
	Girls	43.8	4.7	12.2	4.1	16.5	8.0	1.1	354
Science	Class	47.3	6.8	9.1	0.0	30.5	2.2	2.2	131
	Boys	36.8	4.0	16.5	1.6	23.3	6.4	0.4	416
	Girls	38.2	4.2	18.7	1.5	21.8	4.7	1.0	688
Total	Class	46.0	6.2	7.0	1.8	28.6	1.5	4.8	272
	Boys	40.7	4.2	13.4	3.8	20.9	7.2	1.3	1034
	Girls	39.3	3.8	17.7	3.0	19.8	7.4	0.8	1552

TABLE 16

Number of Pupils Receiving Ten or More Moves Who Received Various Types of Teacher Ratings

Subject	No rating	Positive	Negative	Pos and Neg	f
Mathematics	0	9	0	11	20
Social Studies	1	7	1	10	19
Science	1	9	0	14	24
All Subjects	0	2	0	23	25

Prescribing, permitting, or prohibiting an activity is almost exclusively in the domain of the teacher. Requesting a directive, requesting permission, or responding to a directive tend to be pupil moves. This again reflects the different roles played in the classroom game.

The data in Table 15 indicate that the teachers' directives to boys represent about the same proportion of total instructional moves to boys as is the case with girls. The real differences come when comparing teacher moves to the whole class with teacher moves to individual boys and girls. Prescribing and prohibiting behaviors are more typical of teacher behavior with the whole class. Permitting behavior is more common in individual settings. Individuals request permission and it is to individuals that permission is given. In general talk with the whole class the teacher is more likely to give common guidelines for work and behavior. These guidelines take the form of prescriptions and prohibitions.

MEANINGS IN DIFFERENT LOCATIONS

A major reason for coding locations in this study was to see if there appeared to be any differences in the type of meaning communicated in different settings. The data in Table 17 suggest that the amount of subject matter communicated in a given location varies from teacher to teacher. The only consistent figures are for locations where teachers and pupils are separated. Under this condition the moves almost always have instructional meaning. Generally, the differences between teachers reflected in the above data can be explained by their gross classroom procedures. For instance, two of the social studies sessions were begun by class discussions of the current primary elections and the Vietnam war. Other sessions were begun with remarks that set the stage for individual work.

Pupils in the mathematics class went to the teacher's desk when they needed help on a problem. In such a context substantive meanings were more likely to be communicated than when the teacher went to the pupils' desks to check on their progress. In science and social studies this pattern was reversed. The teachers in these subjects kept cumbersome records on each pupil at their own desks, so it was at the teacher's desk that pupils' progress was checked, and thus a high proportion of instructional meanings communicated.

The chalk board was the only place coded as a media location in the mathematics class. When teacher and pupil went there, it was to work on a problem. Problem-solving usually involves the communication of substantive meanings. In social studies the few moves coded in a media location tended to focus on the use pupils were making of the filmstrip projector rather than on the content of the filmstrip. Again there is inconsistency across classes in the types of meanings communicated in a particular location. This type of inconsistency might be reduced in classes which are structured by the materials from one of the individualized instruction projects.

TABLE 17

Distribution of Meanings Communicated in Different Locations

Location	Mathematics			Social Studies			Science		
	% SUB	% INS	f	% SUB	% INS	f	% SUB	% INS	f
Classroom	6.5	93.4	245	39.5	66.7	180	12.5	87.8	343
T Desk	25.7	75.9	572	7.2	93.5	809	10.5	90.6	1093
P Desk	16.8	85.4	540	24.1	81.5	287	24.6	76.2	617
Media	44.1	62.5	211	7.4	92.6	54	13.5	86.5	59
Other	10.5	92.2	38	19.7	81.7	137	1.7	98.2	116
Separated	4.6	95.3	116	1.9	98.1	158	1.2	98.8	165

MEANINGS IN GROUPS OF DIFFERENT SIZES

Since most of the teacher-pupil interaction in the individualized classes took place in groups of one or two pupils, it is not surprising that the percentages of substantive and instructional moves in these groups are rather close to those for all moves (Table 18). Again in social studies a relatively high percentage of moves in a large group context (5+) have substantive meaning. Here, too, several of the moves (11 percent) have both substantive and instructional meanings. The one category in which the classes vary considerably is that for groups of five or more pupils. This almost always means the whole class. Not surprisingly, these figures are very close to those in the preceding section where the location was the entire class. The explanation of the high percentage of substantive moves in social studies is also the same: the current events discussion involved the whole class with substantive meanings. In the mathematics and science classes the comments to the whole class were most often relevant to what was to be done either in that period or in succeeding periods.

SUMMARY

The role of the teacher in these individualized classes is played out in dealings with individuals or small groups of pupils. It is a game fundamentally different from the lecture-discussion game for the teacher. Its whole purpose has shifted away from giving subject matter to the pupils. For the pupil the game has also changed radically. Subject matter is learned from books, filmstrips, experiments, or other pupils. Time spent with the teacher is a small fraction of the class period. During this time

TABLE 18

Distribution of Meanings Communicated in Groups of Different Size

Group Size	Mathematics			Social Studies			Science		
	% SUB	% INS	f	% SUB	% INS	f	% SUB	% INS	f
1	23.7	78.7	1385	11.0	90.2	1215	10.7	90.1	893
2	19.7	81.7	71	16.2	84.5	148	16.2	84.7	1131
3	0.0	100.0	2	1.5	98.5	67	0.0	100.0	2
4	0.0	100.0	2	11.1	88.9	9	0.0	100.0	11
5+	6.3	94.9	245	40.0	71.1	180	12.5	88.1	344
Uncertain	0.0	100.0	17	0.0	100.0	6	0.0	100.0	12

the teacher is a director of learning, regulator of activity, source of supplies. For most pupils he is not a source of subject matter, although he does serve as a subject-matter resource when something is incomprehensible. When subject matter is communicated it is almost always relevant to the course. Usually, however, the talk between teacher and pupil is about other things: assignments, materials, statements, activities. This talk serves to keep things going in the classroom, supporting and encouraging the learning activity of the pupils, but most of the learning activity takes place apart from the teacher.

SIX

The Data:
Interaction Units

When instruction is individualized, there is a natural unit, usually larger than the move and often larger than Bellack's cycle. This unit is made up of the cluster of moves between teacher and pupil at a particular time. I call it an interaction unit. Its boundaries are generally marked by a change in the composition of the communication group. Exceptions to this are (a) when there is an interruption and (b) when a given group is augmented or decreased but the focus of the discussion is not changed. In the event of an interruption, the moves constituting the interruption form one interaction unit. Those before and after the interruption together constitute one interaction unit. Sometimes, particularly when pupils have been working in pairs, a pupil will be interacting with the teacher and his partner will join them. When this sort of change in group composition does not change the focus of the interaction, only one interaction unit is coded.

The interaction unit may be characterized in a number of ways: by the pupils involved, location, initiator of the interaction, number of moves and the meanings expressed through them, whether the interaction represents an interruption, and so forth. This analysis focuses on the initiator of the interaction, the target, the number of moves, and the meanings communicated. Following Resnick,[1] the analysis will also involve comparison of brief (eight or fewer moves) and extended (nine or more moves) interaction units, as well as of interruptions.

Teacher and pupils. Although the classes studied here were primarily individualized, some communication took place in the total class context. These interaction units were almost always (98 percent of the time) initiated by the teacher (Table 19). In the individualized context, however, it was more common for the pupil to initiate the interaction. Overall, nearly 64 percent of the interaction units were initiated

[1] Lauren B. Resnick, "Teacher Behavior in an Informal British Infant School," *School Review,* Vol. LXXXI (November 1970), pp. 63–83.

by pupils. In mathematics, pupils initiated the interaction 50 percent more often than did the teacher. In social studies they did so 75 percent more often and in science 109 percent more often than did the teacher. Again there is the correlation with the degree of individualization. In mathematics, where the pupils' work was the most structured, they approached the teacher less frequently, and he had more time to approach the pupils himself. The work in science was most individualized and pupils approached the teacher a higher proportion of the time. A possible explanation of this is that when pupils are working on different projects, their questions can less frequently be answered by other pupils than when all are working on the same assignment.

Generally there were more moves in the interactions initiated by the pupils than in those initiated by the teacher. Overall, there were 47 percent more moves in interactions initiated by pupils. Only in social studies were the units initiated by the teacher longer. When pupils initiated the interaction there tended to be more moves with substantive meanings. This was true in each subject. On an average there were 5.5 times more substantive moves in pupil-initiated interactions than in those initiated by the teacher.

Not only do pupils initiate a higher proportion of interactions, they also initiate extended interactions in a higher proportion of their interactions. Thirty-seven percent of pupil-initiated interactions were extended compared to 21 percent for teachers, although these figures vary considerably across subjects. Overall, in the individualized encounters there are 2.2 times as many brief as extended interactions, yet, not surprisingly, there are 2.7 times as many moves in extented interactions as in brief. Thus the majority of the teacher's time with pupils is in interactions with nine or more moves.

It was rare for the teacher to deal with subject matter in the brief interactions he initiated. Rather, he gave directions, inquired how a pupil was progressing, and so forth. Subject matter was more likely to be dealt with in pupil-initiated brief interactions, although this too was uncommon. Brief interactions dealt primarily with such topics as assignments, materials, and procedures.

A move in an extended interaction was more likely to have substantive meaning than one in a brief interaction. In pupil-initiated interactions it was over three times more likely and in teacher-initiated interactions it was over eight times more likely. Although the ratio of substantive to instructional meanings was still low compared to Bellack's classes, the extended interaction was the place for talking about subject matter.

TABLE 19

Interaction Units: Their Moves and Content

			Number of Units			
Subject	Initiator	Target	Brief	Extended	Total	Brief
Mathematics						
	Teacher	Class	28	9	37	0
	Teacher	Boy	35	4	39	0
	Teacher	Girl	34	3	37	1
	Teacher	B & G	79	7	76	1
	Pupil	Class	0	0	0	0
	Boy	Teacher	23	9	32	17
	Girl	Teacher	49	33	82	23
	Pupil	Teacher	72	42	114	40
Social Studies						
	Teacher	Class	4	6	10	0
	Teacher	Boy	33	10	43	0
	Teacher	Girl	15	9	24	0
	Teacher	B & G	48	19	67	0
	Pupil	Class	2	0	2	0
	Boy	Teacher	37	8	45	3
	Girl	Teacher	51	21	72	16
	Pupil	Teacher	88	29	117	19
Science						
	Teacher	Class	21	11	32	0
	Teacher	Boy	21	12	33	0
	Teacher	Girl	25	6	31	3
	Teacher	B & G	46	18	64	3
	Pupil	Class	0	0	0	0
	Boy	Teacher	26	21	47	3
	Girl	Teacher	44	43	87	4
	Pupil	Teacher	70	64	134	7
All Subjects						
	Teacher	Class	53	26	79	0
	Teacher	Boy	89	26	115	0
	Teacher	Girl	74	18	92	4
	Teacher	B & G	163	44	207	4
	Pupil	Class	2	0	2	0
	Boy	Teacher	86	38	124	23
	Girl	Teacher	144	97	241	43
	Pupil	Teacher	230	135	365	66

Substantive Moves			Total Moves			Interruptions	
Extended	Total	Brief	Extended	Total		Brief	Extended
16	16	62	203	265		2	1
5	5	92	70	162		1	0
4	5	116	48	164		3	0
9	10	208	118	326		4	0
0	0	0	0	0		0	0
17	34	103	119	222		5	0
275	298	193	716	909		5	1
292	332	296	835	1131		10	1
72	72	6	174	180		1	0
3	3	108	338	446		3	0
5	5	22	176	198		2	0
8	8	130	514	644		5	0
0	0	3	0	3		0	0
45	48	143	123	266		7	1
88	104	170	365	535		11	2
133	152	313	488	801		18	3
43	43	55	294	349		4	0
39	39	62	187	249		8	0
14	17	49	111	160		5	0
53	56	111	298	409		13	0
0	0	0	0	0		0	0
67	70	109	390	499		6	0
149	153	164	972	1136		6	0
216	223	273	1362	1635		12	0
131	131	123	671	794		7	1
47	47	262	595	857		12	0
23	27	187	335	522		10	0
70	74	449	930	1379		22	0
0	0	3	0	3		0	0
129	152	355	632	987		18	1
512	555	527	2053	2580		22	3
641	707	882	2685	3567		40	4

About one interaction unit in seven was an interruption in teacher-initiated interactions. Pupils interrupted slightly less frequently, about once in every eight interactions. Regardless of initiator, most of the interruptions were brief interactions, although pupils were more likely to start an extended interruption.

The picture of the individualized game emerging at this level is one where most of the talk between teacher and pupil is in extended interactions where it is more likely that subject matter will be dealt with. The probability that subject matter is discussed increases greatly if it is the pupil rather than the teacher who initiates the extended interaction. Although most of the interaction (over 70 percent of all moves) is in extended units, most of the interaction units (over two-thirds) are brief. It is mostly in the brief interactions that the teacher takes care of class maintenance. These interactions are more likely to convey instructional meanings such as pointing out the location of materials, giving permission to leave the room, or disciplining inappropirate behavior.

This sixth-grade class is quite different from the British infant school classes observed by Resnick. There he found a much more rapid rate of interaction, a much greater proportion of substantive moves in the extended interactions, and a far higher proportion of interruptions, particularly in pupil-initiated units where over half were interruptions.[2] These differences are probably related to the instructional formats as well as to the ages of the pupils. The infant school environment is far richer in materials. The teacher analyzes what a pupil can do, then he guides his learning by posing substantive questions relative to the materials. In the sixth grades studied, much of the work was more structured: learning was guided by instruction sheets, books, and filmstrips, and understanding was checked through the pupils' written work. The teacher did not need to keep as close a check on the pupil and there was, generally, less need for substantive interaction.

Boys, girls, and teacher. The analysis of interaction units contains the reason for the great difference in activity of boys and girls. The average girl initiates far more interaction with the teacher than does the average boy (Table 20). When corrections are made for the actual amount of time spent in the room by boys and girls, the average girl initiated 2.5 times as many interactions with the teacher than did the average boy. In social studies the figure was 1.84 and in science 1.46. Moreover, in each subject the interactions initiated by girls have more moves than those initiated by boys. Interestingly, the teacher offsets this imbalance to some extent. After corrections for the actual time in class,

[2] *Ibid.*

TABLE 20

Number of Interaction Units per Day in Class for Average Boy and Girl

Subject	Pupil Initiated		Teacher Initiated	
	By Boys	By Girls	To Boys	To Girls
Mathematics	.86	2.16	1.05	.97
Social studies	1.02	1.88	.98	.63
Science	.90	1.31	.63	.47
All subjects	.93	1.69	.86	.64

each teacher initiates more interactions with boys than with girls, and these interactions with boys tend to have more moves in them than those initiated with girls. In each subject the teacher initiates more extended interactions with boys than with girls and in each subject girls initiate more than twice as many extended interactions as do boys. Not only do girls initiate more and longer interactions than do boys, but there are also a larger number of substantive moves in their interactions. Generally this is due to a higher proportion of substantive moves, not simply more moves per interaction.

Teacher and individual pupil. On an individual basis we see the same kind of range in activity with interaction units as we saw with moves. At one extreme was a boy who initiated only one interaction during the three weeks of observation. At the other extreme was a girl who initiated 28 interactions over this period with no fewer than nine in any subject. Only one of the girls failed to initiate at least one inter-action unit with each teacher. Seven of the boys did so, and three of these failed to initiate interaction with two of the three teachers.

Summary. This analysis of interaction units completes the picture of individualized instruction. It helps explain the inequality of teacher interaction with boys and girls in the classes observed. In those instances when the teacher initiated interaction there were more interactions with boys than with girls, and more moves with boys than with girls. It appears that girls had more activity with the teacher because they initiated con-siderably more interaction than did the boys, and there were more moves in the interactions initiated by the girls.

SEVEN
The Individualized Game: A Summary

The metaphor of the language game has given shape to this study as to Bellack's. It also provides a framework for understanding the results presented in Chapters 3 through 6. In this section the results will be reinterpreted in terms of classroom activity as a game in which the participants make moves which may be described by certain general rules. A major focus for this discussion is provided by the question: how does the game change when the number of players changes? That is, is there a difference between the rules describing interactions in the individualized game and the rules describing interactions when the game involves all class members?

The classroom game is characterized by several attributes, and changes as these attributes change. Like all games, it has players. These players have various positions in the game and their range of activity within the game is determined to a considerable extent by their respective positions. The classroom game is characterized by its setting. The fact that it takes place within a classroom within a school is probably the most important factor in determining its form. The setting makes it an educational game with its own particular criteria for "winning." The goals are particular kinds of changes in the pupil participants. The roles taken and the activities performed are to this end.

It is within the context of the school and its general goals that the individuality of the participants gives distinctive aspects to individual games. Within the school, all classrooms are obviously not the same. The laboratory provides a different context than does the lecture hall. Within the classroom too there is a variety of behavior settings. Each of these may have an impact on the type of game being played. Different locations have these effects, when they do, largely because of the different objects within them. The confluence of participants, locations, and objects affects the activity which constitutes the game. Thus the game in which the teacher helps two pupils adjust the overhead projector to be able to trace a leaf is a different game from that in which two pupils are working on a report.

When instruction is individualized there are several concurrent games in the classroom, each involving different players in different settings. There is the game played by the teacher and the pupils with whom he is in communication. There are other games played by individual pupils and small groups of pupils. These games include making reports, tracing maps, watching filmstrips, working problems, taking tests, and devising and executing experiments. In this analysis of individualized instruction, only the games participated in by both teacher and pupil have been studied.

Rules Describing Player Activity

Like other games, the classroom game is to some extent guided by rules for appropriate behavior among the various categories of participants. Bellack stated the rules for his lecture-discussion game.[1] Here a comparable set of rules is given for the individualized game involving teacher and pupil. First we will look at gross activity.

(1) There are different ways to look at a player's activity. For instance there is the relative number of moves made by the various players and categories of players. As a group, teachers made 56 percent of all moves, pupils 44 percent. In terms of gross activity, the teachers dominated the game. The pupils, of course, did not constitute a homogeneous group. Girls were much more active participants, making 70 percent more moves than boys, on the average.

Data on groups are interesting, but the individualized game is played by individuals and at that level the generalizations break down. Some pupils are more active than teachers in encounters, others much less active. Some pupils make and receive many times more moves in their interaction with teachers than do their classmates. There are no rules to describe the relative amounts of activity of individual pupils and teachers.

(2) There is a second measure of activity in the individualized classes. It is the number of times a teacher and pupil interact, that is, the number of interaction units. In terms of this measure, girls get together with the teacher to talk 39 percent more often than do boys. Regardless of the measure of activity, we can state that sixth-grade girls have more interactions with male teachers than do sixth-grade boys.

---

[1] Arno A. Bellack *et al., The Language of the Classroom* (New York: Teachers College Press, 1966), ch. 9.

The generalization certainly does not hold on the individual level where some boys interact with the teacher much more often than some girls do.

(3) A game may be characterized not only by the relative activity of different players, but also by the pace at which the game is played. In Bellack's classes approximately six moves per minute were made. In our individualized classes moves were made at more than twice this rate. This is especially surprising because often there were periods in the individualized classes where there was no teacher-pupil interaction. In our two lecture-discussion classes the pace was three times that in Bellack's classes, with 19.4 moves per minute. Part of these differences is accounted for by our coding of non-verbal moves. Still, it seems that a determining factor in the pace of the game is the participants, particularly the age of the pupils, rather than the mode of instruction.

Rules Describing Player Functions

Amount of activity and pace are the grosser characteristics of a game. Finer analysis focuses on the moves that are made and what they accomplish. A first level of this analysis is concerned with the way different players function. The functional unit in the classroom game is the pedagogical move, of which there are four types: structuring, soliciting, responding, and reacting. The following rules give a picture of how these functions are carried out.

(1) The roles of various participants in the game are revealed by their relative use of the various moves. The teacher makes three-fourths of the soliciting moves. This is somewhat less than the six-sevenths reported by Bellack, yet it remains true that the soliciting role is usually the teacher's. Similarly the responding role in the individualized class belongs to the pupil. The pupil makes about five-sixths of the responses in this study compared to six-sevenths in Bellack's. Soliciting and responding are even more at the heart of the individualized game than of the lecture-discussion game. These two moves account for 71 percent of all moves compared to 63 percent in Bellack's classes.

It has already been noted that girls play a more active part in the game than do boys. They make almost twice as many soliciting moves and half again as many responding moves than do boys. They are far more likely to initiate interaction with the teacher, and the teacher is somewhat more likely to solicit them. This difference in boy and girl figures may be characteristic of an individualized game played by sixth-graders. However, in the lecture-discussion game with the same players the girls made soliciting moves only 26 percent more often than the boys, while responding 41 percent more often.

The real differences in roles are seen at the individual level. Some pupils are far more active in terms of initiating interaction, some are relatively passive; some determine to a relatively high degree what takes place between teacher and pupil, others do so minimally. These extremes occur to a greater extent in individuals, but continue to be evident across subjects. One pupil solicited the teacher in only eight percent of his moves, another in 43 percent. One pupil was responding to the teacher in 87 percent of his moves, another in only 26 percent. These differences in pupil role are matched by corresponding differences in the roles teachers take with different pupils, for teacher and pupil activity are complementary.

(2) Interaction units are more frequently initiated by the pupils than by the teacher in the individualized interactions. That is, the sequence of moves between a teacher and pupil tends to occur at the pleasure of the pupil. This is in marked contrast to interaction units involving the whole class, which are nearly always initiated by the teacher. Girls initiate almost twice as many interaction units with the teacher as do boys. Their interaction units are longer, too. These two facts explain why girls give and receive so many more moves than the boys.

(3) A structuring move sets the context for a game or part of a game. In the individualized class a sub-game is begun each time the teacher starts working with a new pupil or group of pupils. Thus there are many more opportunities for a structuring move than in the normal lecture-discussion game. Moreover, since it is often the pupil who determines the topic of interaction with the teacher, the pupil has more occasion to make structuring moves. The individualized games are typically launched by a soliciting move rather than a structuring move, but the pupils launch these games via a structuring move sufficiently often to be equal with the teacher in terms of the number of structuring moves made. Half the structuring in these classes is done by the pupil. Here is further evidence that the individualized game is a very different kind of game from that described by Bellack. The pupil, even though only in the sixth grade, has more responsibility for structuring his interaction with the teacher. For these individualized classes, six percent of pupil moves were structuring. Fewer than one percent of pupil moves were structuring in Bellack's study.

(4) A reacting move is reflexive in nature. The prior verbal or non-verbal activity of another player serves as the occasion for the react-

ing move. The recovery of a fumble or the applause of the crowd are counterparts in sports to reacting in the classroom game. Like the fumble recovery, a reacting move may be a part of the ongoing play or, like fan reaction, it can convey a rating of the preceding activity. In order for a classroom player to react in the latter way he must be able to stand somewhat outside the game, rating the individual moves, as well as be able to participate in the game. He has a dual role of player and spectator. Bellack reported in his study that ratings were made almost exclusively by the teacher. Reactions which continue the development or modification of the topic, being optional in nature, represent greater player initiative than the other reflexive move, responding. Reacting in this mode too is more typical of the teacher. In Bellack's classes teachers made four-fifths of all reacting moves. An even greater proportion was made by the teacher in the lecture-discussion classes of this study. However, teachers made only two-thirds of the reacting moves in the individualized classes, a further indication of the different nature of the individualized game.

(5) The pedagogical move can have different forms. Typically the meaning communicated through the move is fully present in the words spoken, although redundant gestures may accompany these words. About six-sevenths of the teacher's moves have the form of speaking. This is true for both initiatory and reflexive moves. Most of the remaining moves are those in which a gesture accompanies the speaking and is necessary for the full communication of meaning. A little over five-eighths of pupil-initiatory moves and three-fourths of pupil-reflexive moves have the form of speaking. Gesturing provides part or all of the meaning in almost all the remaining moves. Over one-eighth of pupil-initiatory moves and one-sixth of pupil-reflexive moves are made solely through a gesture. The greater role of gesturing in pupil moves may be indicative of the difference in verbal ability among players, as well as their role differences.

RULES FOR MEANINGS COMMUNICATED

When players make their various moves, they do so in order to communicate meanings to one another. This is at the heart of the linguistic game. The individualized classes in this study have their own particular rules as to what sort of meaning is communicated and by whom.

(1) Regardless of whether the individualized game was played in mathematics, science, or social studies, the major part of the game is played with instructional meanings. The player in the role of teacher is

concerned with the progress a pupil is making, indicating what a pupil is to do, ascertaining that the pupil understands what is expected of him, and rating a pupil's work. The pupil is concerned with procuring supplies and materials, determining what is expected of him, and gaining approval of what he has done. Clearly the content has to be communicated through the materials. The teacher-pupil game was not directed primarily toward the communication of subject matter. Fewer than one-sixth of the moves conveyed substantive meaning. This distinguishes this individualized game in a most radical way from the lecture-discussion game.

(2) When a substantive move is made in the individualized game it is almost always relevant to the individualized topic. At most one-sixteenth of the substantive moves were off the topic in any of the classes. This is interesting because one would assume that the individualized format gives the teacher and pupil more latitude in exploring substantive areas not directly related to the work at hand. It is in Bellack's lecture-discussion classes, however, that one finds as many as one-eighth of the substantive moves dealing with areas other than that under study. The relatively small amount of time that the teacher is in contact with a given pupil in the individualized class may constrain his substantive discourse in a way not felt by the teacher in the lecture-discussion class, who is theoretically in communication with all pupils for the full period.

(3) In terms of the logic of the move, over five-sixths of the substantive moves involve empirical processes. When the preliminary class discussions are removed from the social studies data, only one-fiftieth of the substantive moves involve evaluative processes. Again it might have been expected that the individualized setting would allow for more expression and examination of opinion than in the total class format, but the fraction of substantive evaluative moves is one-third that found in Bellack's classes. The individualized format in these classes did not have a freeing effect on the type of substance dealt with, or on the way in which it was handled.

(4) In the individualized game most moves convey instructional meaning. Of these, three-sevenths focus on some aspect of the work the pupil is to do: the teacher-pupil game is often played out in relation to what, for the pupil, is the primary game—his interaction with the learning materials. A much smaller number of moves relate to the objects which the pupil is to use in his other game. Only one-seventh of the instructional moves focus on materials.

(5) There is a subset of instructional moves which convey explicit directives. A player is told to do something, he indicates what he will do,

or he asks for permission or directions. The activity may take place within the immediate pupil-teacher game or, more often, in another game. In five-sixths of the teacher's directives a pupil is told to do something. In most of the pupil moves with directive meaning, the pupil is seeking permission or directions for something he is to do himself. In one-sixth of these pupil moves, however, the pupil actually directs teacher activity. Unlike Bellack's classes, many of these moves request non-verbal behavior. Fewer than one-eighth of the pupil directives to a teacher request the teacher to repeat an utterance. It appears that pupil expectations about teacher behavior in the individualized classes are not the same as expectations in Bellack's classes.

(6) In the individualized game between teacher and pupil two-thirds of the instructional moves have logical meanings and one-third have extra-logical meanings. That is, one-third are related to directives. A relatively large part of this game focuses on what players are to do. Of the moves involving logical processes, one-fifth are ratings and three-fourths involve empirical processes. There is little discussion of instructional topics in evaluative terms. The fraction of moves involving evaluative processes other than ratings, one-fiftieth, is the same found by Bellack. In these classes the individualized format has not affected the amount of evaluative talk about instructional matters.

(7) Nearly half the reacting moves conveyed a positive, negative, or qualifying rating. One-fourth of the pupil reactions and three-fifths of the teacher reactions were ratings. From another perspective, one-sixth of the rating was done by pupils. Rating is primarily but not exclusively a teacher function. In Bellack's game pupils rarely reacted by rating the moves of other participants. In the individualized game it is not rare for a pupil to rate a teacher move.

The notion that boys and girls represent different classes of pupil players gains support from the way the teacher rates them. For girls the ratio of positive to negative ratings by the teacher was twice that for the boys.

(8) There do not appear to be any rules describing where the teacher-pupil interaction occurs, at least not in terms of the location categories used in this study. There is only one clear rule describing a type of meaning communicated in a particular type of location: when the teacher and pupil are separated, it is almost always an instructional meaning that is communicated. Probably in individualized classes where formalized materials give greater structure to the activities, differences of meanings conveyed in particular locations are more evident.

The Teacher-Pupil Game

The game played by the teacher in the individualized class is very different from the one he plays in the lecture-discussion class. But this game is not the only classroom game; it is one of several. From the pupil's point of view the individualized game with the teacher may have characteristics of a pre-game strategy session with the coach or of a post-game viewing of the game films to analyze the strong and weak points of one's play. For the pupil, this game played with the teacher is not the real classroom game. The real game is more often a solitary one, where the pupil deals with the learning materials or, as in the science classes, a game where a few pupils work together toward the prescribed outcomes.

THE SYSTEM

It is evident from the complexity of the analytic system and the amount of time required for coding it that, as it stands, it is not generally useful. The system provides the data for several studies, not just one. The results presented in Chapters 3 through 6 were selected results. No sequential analysis was carried out. Analysis of relationships between categories was carried out in only a few instances. Nevertheless there are important characteristics of the system and distinctions made within the system that should be of value for future research efforts.

It is of primary importance that the pedagogical move proved itself to be a highly reliable unit for analyzing teacher-pupil interactions in a situation where (1) both verbal and non-verbal interactions were considered, and (2) the instructional situation was quite different from others in which the move had previously been used. Furthermore, the move lends itself to the coding of contextual variables which in turn allow for the construction of a unit, here called the interaction unit, that gives a suggestive overall picture of what is happening between pupil and teacher when instruction is individualized.

Secondly, the concept of move form provides a way of looking at a particular type of non-verbal behavior, namely behavior which functions as one of the four moves. It is evident that this in no way deals with the affective effect of non-verbal communications. In fact, gestures and expressions which communicate acceptance, rejection, happiness, anxiety, and so forth are not considered because they do not perform the sort of cognitive function considered here. What this way of dealing with non-verbal behavior does is provide a way of partitioning off a particular subset of non-verbal behavior: that which communicates cognitive, in the sense of substantive or instructional, meaning.

The concepts of substantive and instructional meaning were developed in *The Language of the Classroom*. It has become evident in this study that it is worthwhile to look at communications simply in terms of whether they contain substantive and/or instructional meaning, not going beyond this into a set of substantive and a set of instructional categories. I have found that it is possible to go into a classroom and directly code the emitter (as teacher, boy, girl, or group), the pedagogical move, and whether the meaning is substantive or instructional. This was done through number codes which result in a three-digit number for each move. This kind of collapsing of the system results in an instrument both easy to use and informative.

Finally, breaking instructional meanings into the dichotomous categories of directive and non-directive may be a convenient way of looking at classes, particularly at the early elementary levels, where more immediate direction of activities is often thought to be necessary.

EIGHT
Implications

The limited sample used in this study meant that there could be no statistical test of the significance of the results. These results do, however, suggest future research in two major areas: boy-girl differences and individualized instruction.

This study was not initially focused on behavior differences between boys and girls. It was a study of individualized instruction, but it soon became evident that to give a better picture of what was happening in the classes it was necessary to examine boy-girl differences. The resulting description raises several questions. Do similar differences exist in other sixth-grade classes where considerable responsibility is placed upon the pupils to initiate interactions? Do similar differences exist in all sixth-grade classes? The three teachers in this study were male. Is teacher gender an important factor in explaining the initiatory activity of girls relative to that of boys? This series of questions should be repeated for different grade levels and different cultural conditions. Research of this nature can be carried out without expensive recording equipment. Emitter gender and pedagogical move can be coded directly. If it seems necessary to have some measure of the length of moves, then audio tape recording may well be required. However, the question can be answered adequately through research based on live coding of emitter and move.

The second area for research suggested by this study is that of individualized instruction. The sample analyzed here is quite limited. It is limited in terms of the number of teachers in each subject area, in terms of grade level, and in the type of individualization attempted and the supporting materials available for the teacher. Future research should analyze other classes where teachers are individualizing instruction using their own resources and compare these to classes where one of the individualized programs has been implemented with all its supporting materials. It should compare structured individualization to the open classroom. It should analyze individualization at different grade levels.

It should analyze classes where pupils have had previous experience with individualized instruction. It should analyze different modes of individualization: individualization of attention, pace, materials, or combinations of these. Analysis of these different contexts and conditions of individualization could be studied profitably at the simplified level of emitter, move type, and the substantive/instructional dichotomy. It would be interesting to find out whether classes where a formal program of individualization has been implemented have substantive/instructional meaning ratios similar to classes where the teacher is the source of the program. It would also be interesting to see if in other individualized classes the use of various move types is more evenly distributed than in lecture-discussion classes, that is, to see if the roles of teacher and pupil really do shift under this mode of instruction.

CLASSROOM PRACTICE

The results reported here raise questions for the classes studied and, to the extent that similar results are found generally, for those who are considering the use of an individualized approach. The major question concerns the role of the teacher. In these classes the teacher has functioned primarily as one who directs and monitors a pupil's work rather than as one who communicates subject matter to the pupil. This means it is the pupil's responsibility to gather information for himself and deliver it to the teacher for approval rather than to receive and give information to the teacher and his peers in a group context. There are attractive features in both formats. It may be that some combination is desirable.

If, as the results of this study indicate, the role of the teacher is quite different under the two modes of instruction, then the abilities, disposition, and training of the teacher are relevant factors in his decision to operate within one mode or the other or both. What may prove to be liberating for one may be tension-filled for another. The same may be said for the pupil. Certainly the amount of direction and discipline needed to work alone varies among pupils. In the classes observed in this study some of the pupils were easily distracted and spent little time on their work. Others proceeded with a minimum of help from the teacher. If one is to consider the implications for teachers, pupils, and instructional goals of changing to another mode of instruction, then the decision cannot be a hasty one.

*   *   *   *   *

It is hoped that the results of this study will stimulate further study into teacher and pupil factors relevant to individualization, as well as into what goes on between teacher and pupil in that context.

Appendix

CODING INSTRUCTIONS [1]

1. General Coding Instructions

   1.1. Coding is from the viewpoint of the observer, with pedagogical meaning inferred from the emitter's behavior.

   1.2. Grammatical form may give a clue, but is not decisive in coding. For example, soliciting may be found in declarative, interrogative or imperative form. Likewise, responding may be in the form of a question, frequently indicating tentativeness on the part of the speaker.

   1.3. All missed statements and all non-codable statements (e.g., er, ah, mmm, well . . ., etc.) are coded in the emitter, move (not codable), and move context categories alone. Partially missed statements are fully coded only if there is enough information to code the pedagogical move, the substantive and substantive-logical meaning, and/or the instructional and instructional-logical meaning. Those moves immediately following a move that is not codable are coded as usual, if the context is clear and unambiguous. If alternative codes are clearly possible, code the move as not codable for these moves too.

2. Pedagogical Moves

   2.1. A soliciting move begins with the first manifestly educative statement and ends with:

      a. The end of the utterance

---

[1] The coding instructions given in Bellack's *The Language of the Classroom* have been incorporated into these instructions.

b. The beginning of a structuring, responding, or reacting move.

2.2. Solicitations that request permission to speak have instructional meaning and directive meaning. They are coded in the extra-logical category of requesting permission (RPR).

P: Mr. M.?   SOL/ . . . /RPR
T: Yes?   SOL/ . . . /PER

P: (Hand raised)   SOL/ . . . /RPR
T: Ellen?   SOL/ . . . /PER

2.3. Solicitations which give permission to speak have instructional meaning and directive meaning. They are coded in the extra-logical category of permitting a performance (PER). The agent is the target (see examples for 2.2).

2.4   Tentative, optional, and required assignments as well as clarification of an assignment are coded as soliciting moves with directive meaning.

P: What should I do now?   SOL/. . . ./DIR

T: Do pages 30 and 31.   SOL/. . . ./PRE

2.5. When checking statements (e.g., "Follow me?" "Get it?") occur within a structuring or reacting move, soliciting is not coded unless there is a pause or verbal cue indicating that a response is expected. Such statements when they occur within a larger move do not appear as part of the code for the larger move. When the checking statements expect a response, they will be coded as having instructional, non-directive, meaning.

T: O.K.?   SOL/ . . . /ACC/FAC

2.6. Implicit in any solicitation are the concepts of knowing or not knowing, doing or not doing. Therefore code "responding" for any one of the range of possible responses (including invalid ones), and also for any reply referring to knowing or not knowing, agreeing to do or refusing to do. The physical response to a directive will be coded as a responding move. However, in the case of responding to the directive to speak, the meaning of the utterance will be coded, not the fact that the respondent is complying with the directive to speak.

2.7 Occasionally a teacher or student responds to a soliciting move with a question. Coding in these instances is in terms of context and intent. For example, students frequently respond with a question to indicate the tentativeness of their responses. These are coded as responding moves. If, however, the "responding" question is a genuine solicitation (i.e., it expects a response), it is coded as a soliciting move.

2.8. A solicitation which calls for a fact is coded as fact-stating, but if the response gives both a fact and an explanation, the logical meaning of the response is coded as explaining.

2.9. A solicitation which calls for an opinion is coded as opining, but if the response gives both an opinion and a justification, the logical meaning of the response is coded as justifying.

2.10. Responses to a directive are coded in two ways.

a. When the response is an indication of intent to carry out or not to carry out the directed activity it is coded in the non-directive instructional meaning category of statement (STA) and the instructional logical category of compliance (COM), alternative (ALT), or non-compliance (NCM).

b. When the response is the actual carrying out of the directed activity it is coded in the appropriate directive instructional meaning category (usually ACT, ACV, or ACP) and in the instructional logical category of compliance (COM).

2.11. A speaker cannot respond to his own solicitation. (1) If the speaker answers his own question immediately after asking it, the question is taken to be rhetorical and a stylistic device rather than a true SOL. (2) If a speaker answers his own question after an intervening incorrect answer, the correct answer to the solicitation is coded as a reaction to the incorrect answer, since the purpose of the question was not to elicit a response from the questioner. (3) If a speaker answers his own question after a pause, the answer is coded as a reaction, indicating that the speaker is primarily reacting to the absence of an expected response. (4) If the speaker, through his own action immediately following the solicitation, acquires the information requested in the solicitation, the solicitation will not be considered to be a true solicitation. The composite activity of soliciting and acquiring information is considered as a structuring move.

2.12. A reaction begins at the beginning of an utterance or following a non-verbal response or the absence of an expected move. A reaction is still in progress when the speaker:

a. Evaluates or otherwise discusses a previous move.

b. Rephrases a previous move or makes reference to it.

c. Expands a previous move by stating its implications, interpreting it, or drawing conclusions from the same point or sub-point.

A reacting move ends when any of the following occurs:

a. The utterance ends.

b. A solicitation begins.

c. The speaker indicates the end of the reaction by some verbal convention, such as, "All right, now let's turn to. . . ."

d. A distinct (not parenthetic) shift occurs to another substantive area not heretofore mentioned or not under immediate discussion.

e. A distinct (not parenthetic) shift occurs from any substantive category to an instructional category not heretofore mentioned or under immediate discussion.

2.13. A reaction to a solicitation occurs only when the reaction is about the solicitation (i.e., "That's a good question") and not a response to the solicitation.

3. Move Form

3.1. Non-verbal and/or non-oral behavior is coded as a move only when it performs a function in classroom communication. Writing, gesturing, or manipulating materials is coded only when it structures, solicits, serves as a response, or a reaction.

3.2. When a move is communicated through speaking accompanied by gesturing it is coded as follows:

a. Speaking: The non-verbal aspects of the communication add nothing to the cognitive meaning conveyed by the verbal communication.

b. Speaking and gesturing: Cognitive meanings, in addition to those conveyed by the words, are communicated through bodily movements, usually pointing.

3.3.   Only cognitive meanings expressed through a gesture are coded. No attempt is made to code emotional meanings communicated through a gesture.

3.4.   When a pupil goes to the teacher, hands a paper to the teacher, and waits (and when these actions are not in response to a teacher directive), the pupil will be considered to be soliciting the teacher to perform an activity. The prescribed activity is signing a paper if the paper is a library pass, reading the paper if it is the pupil's work. The teacher's non-oral response of reading or writing is seen as a responding move complying with the pupil's directive. The form of the pupil's solicitation is gesturing (GES). The form of the teacher's response is writing (WRI).

3.5.   Pupil hand-raising will be coded as a move whose form is the gesture when (1) the hand-raising occasions a teacher move, or (2) the hand-raising serves as a response. When hand-raising is not a response, it will be coded as a soliciting move through which the pupil requests permission to speak. The teacher move occasioned by the hand raising ("Yes?" or nodding the head or pointing to the pupil, etc.) is also a solicitation permitting the pupil performance.

3.6.   There are several ways other than hand-raising that a pupil indicates to the teacher that he wishes to speak to him. These ways include going to the teacher and standing beside him expectantly, gazing at the teacher with a puzzled or troubled expression, shaking one's head "no." These gestures will not be coded as moves.

3.7.   Even when the pupil is out of camera range, there are cues which indicate whether the pupil has initiated the interchange by raising his hand or whether the teacher initiates the interchange by calling on a pupil who has not volunteered. Clues indicating that the pupil has raised his hand include: the interaction is embedded in a series of interactions where the other pupils have raised their hands; the teacher uses the same soliciting form used for others who have had their hands raised; the pupil readily speaks with little initial stumbling; the pupil's move is an initiatory move (this is usually a sufficient although not a necessary cue); the teacher gives signs of "noticing" the pupil. When such cues are present, the pupil will be coded as having made the initiatory move of raising his hand.

4. Communication Group

4.1. The communication group consists of those pupils with whom the teacher is intentionally communicating. The communication group size is coded according to the number of pupils involved in it. When this number is four or fewer, the pupils in the group are identified.

4.2. When two or more pupils are working together, they will (both) all be considered part of the communication group when speaking with the teacher provided that (1) they are all together in the same physical location, and (2) working on the same problems, project, or exercises. Cues indicating that pupils are working together include: explicit and implicit statements to that effect; pupils gathered in a setting apart from other pupils, often around an instructional device such as a map, film strip projector, or blackboard; sharing materials and assisting one another; and (both) all talking to the teacher at the same meeting.

4.3. When one member of a group working together is singled out by the teacher for discipline or some other reason, all group members will be considered to be in the communication group. Only the one singled out is the target.

4.4. When a pupil is not in the group communicating with the teacher but is in a position of overhearing the communication, he is not coded as part of the communication group.

4.5. If a communication group is interrupted by someone from outside the group speaking to the teacher, the initial communication group members will not be coded as part of the group that includes the teacher and interrupter.

4.6. If an interchange with an individual pupil is embedded in communication directed to a group of five or more pupils, the communication group for the interchange with the one pupil will generally be coded as the group of five or more. However, if during the interchange with the individual the rest of the group is engaged in some other activity, then the communication group will be coded as just involving the one pupil.

4.7. When the teacher is talking to the teacher aide, or someone from outside the room, and the communication is not meant for the pupils in the class, the communication group size is coded as zero (0). This indicates that there are no pupils from the class involved in the communication group.

4.8. A cluster of pupil responses, all elicited by the same solicitation, will be considered as one group response (with "multiple emitters" coded in the emitter category) when the various emitters are not asked individually for their responses.

4.9. The target consists of those pupils within the communication group and/or the teacher to whom the move is directed. The target is coded according to its size and, when it contains four or fewer persons, the identity of the targets.

4.10. When the teacher is the emitter, all pupils in the communication group are coded as targets, except in the following cases:

a. The teacher gives a directive to a group member that could not involve other members either because one pupil is specified by name, or there is only one pupil involved in the activity the teacher is trying to control. The target here consists of the one pupil.

b. The teacher specifies who is to talk by name, pronoun, or so phrasing a SOL that one specific person could appropriately respond. Target is the one pupil.

c. The teacher rates a statement or action which is clearly a pupil's own rather than a group product which he is reporting. The target is the one pupil.

d. When a communication group is augmented by a new pupil breaking in with a new topic, he will be considered the target of the teacher utterances dealing with this topic.

However if the other pupils take up the topic, they, too, will be considered targets of the teacher's moves.

4.11. When a pupil is the emitter, his target will be coded as the teacher except in the following cases:

    a. Another pupil is named or otherwise clearly indicated as the one who is to respond. The target is the indicated pupil.

    b. The initiatory move to which a pupil responds or reacts was uttered by another pupil. Code the teacher and the initiating pupil as targets.

    c. If a pupil's communication elicits laughter or some other group reaction, it will be assumed that the target is the entire communication group excepting the emitter.

4.12. When an emitter directs part of a move to one target, part to another, each part is coded as one move. The target must remain constant for any one move.

5. Communication Group Location

5.1. The location coded is the location of the communication group at the beginning of the move, whether or not that location shifts during the move.

5.2. When a communication group is established and the teacher's attention is drawn to a pupil outside the group and physically separated from it, the location of that pupil will be coded as long as he is the target of the teacher's moves, or the emitter of a move.

5.3. Regardless of how close the pupil's desk is to that of the teacher, as long as the pupil remains at his desk and the teacher remains at his, the teacher and pupil will be considered to be separated and the location coded as separated (SEP).

5.4. Media location is coded preferentially to T desk or P desk. Thus if the pupil is using a film strip projector or other piece of apparatus at his desk or the teacher's, the location will be coded as a media location.

5.5. Often media such as blackboards or maps are close to the teacher's desk. If the location is being coded as "teacher's desk," begin coding "media location" when the use of the media begins, whether or not the pupil moves from the teacher's desk. Resume coding teacher's desk only if the use of the media ceases and there is a shift of topic, or if the pupil and teacher move elsewhere.

6. Substantive Meanings

6.1. Substantive meaning is coded for those moves which communicate subject matter, whether that subject matter is appropriate to the lesson being studied or not. There are the following cases, however, where meanings relevant to the subject are communicated but the move is coded as having instructional meaning:

a. An interpretation is requested and given for a statement made by someone in the classroom.

b. An evaluation of a pupil's work or answer is requested or given.

c. There is a communication *about* subject matter (e.g., whether one has studied it, knows it, would like to study it) but not of the subject matter.

6.2. The substantive context of moves with instructional meaning only will not be coded. No substantive categories will be coded for moves with instructional meaning alone.

6.3. If a move has both substantive and instructional meanings, it will be fully coded in both instructional and substantive categories.

7. Substantive-Logical Meanings

7.1. Only when defining is the main focus is a move coded as defining. When the definition is within the immediate context of other substantive-logical meanings, defining is not coded.

7.2. Responses giving facts within the context of an explanatory move or in a sequence of explanatory moves are coded explaining except when the solicitation which elicits the fact-stating clearly calls for a fact, not an explanation. In the latter case, both the solicitation and the response are coded fact-stating.

7.3. "Reverse" definitions, which give the definition and call for the term, are coded as defining moves.

7.4. When more than one substantive-logical process occurs within a single pedagogical move, code according to the following order of priority:

Justifying
Explaining
Opining
Fact-stating
Interpreting
Defining

7.5. An incorrect statement intended as the description of a state of affairs, such as, "The Nile originates in Egypt" would be coded as fact-stating even though it is empirically incorrect.

8. Instructional Meanings

8.1. Occasionally reference is made to more than one of the instructional meaning categories within the same move. In coding, identify the primary instructional function of the move, or its primary focus, and code appropriately.

8.2. Use the following order of precedence when more than one of the instructional categories are involved and the main intent of the discourse cannot be readily determined:

Statement
Logical Process
Assignment
Materials
Procedure
Person
Vocal Action
Physical Action
Cognitive Action—cognition
Emotional Action
General Action
Language Mechanics

8.3. Cognitive Action/Fact-stating is coded when the cognitive process is the main intent of the move.

T: Remember that?

T: Do you know how to . . . ?

8.4. Cognitive Action/Fact-stating is *not* coded when the reference to a cognitive process is incidental. Often this type of reference to thinking or believing is made in order to modify the strength of the claim one is making.

P: I think the answer is 32.

8.5. Both Cognitive Action/Fact-stating and the substantive/substantive-logical meanings are coded when the move gives them approximately equal prominence.

P: I don't know for sure, but I think that would be 52.

9. Instructional-Logical Meanings

9.1 Logical meanings

a. Interpreting (INT) is coded as instructional-logical meaning for clarifying solicitations and responses in which the speaker asks for or gives the referent or antecedent in a previous move.

P: We went there yes-
    terday.
T: To the library?   /SOL/ . . . /STA/INT
P: Yes.   /RES/ . . . /STA/INT

If the emitter requests or gives a clarifying response involving the definition of terms, code defining.

b. When a statement with substantive meaning is qualified, this is considered a qualifying rating of that statement. The qualification often contains more substantive information, in which case the move is coded as having substantive and instructional meaning.

9.2. Extra-Logical Meanings

a. All moves which indicate to the target what he is to do, what he may do, or what he may not do are directives. When they do not convey subject matter, they are coded in instructional meaning categories of ACV, ACP, ACC,

ACE, or ACT and in the Instructional-Logical categories, PRE, PER, PRO, RPT.

b. All moves in which the emitter seeks to learn what he is to do or seeks permission to do what he wants to do have directive meaning. When they do not request that subject matter be conveyed, they are coded along the instructional dimension of Agent and in the Instructional-Logical categories, DIR, RPR.

c. When a pupil asks about an assignment, he often is trying to find out what precisely he has to do and/or on what schedule he must do it. In such solicitations he is in fact requesting a directive. The Instructional-Logical dimension is coded (DIR), asking to be directed. When the teacher's next move repeats, clarifies, or interprets the assignment it is with the expectation that the pupil will then respond with the appropriate assignment-fulfilling activities. Thus the teacher's move is a solicitation with extra-logical meaning. It is generally coded as prescribing a performance (PRE).

P: Do I do both of these?   SOL/ . . . /ASG/DIR

T: Yes.   SOL/ . . . /ASG/PRE

d. The response to a directive may be of two types: it may consist of whatever activities are necessary to fulfill the directive, or it may consist of a move indicating the intention to fulfill the directive (or not to fulfill it). The coding of these responses is given in section 2.10 of the instructions.

Bibliography

Bellack, Arno A., Herbert M. Kliebard, Ronald T. Hyman, and Frank L. Smith, Jr. *The Language of the Classroom.* New York: Teachers College Press, 1966.

Gibbons, Maurice. *Individualized Instruction.* New York: Teachers College Press, 1971.

Honigman, Fred K. and James Stephens. "Student Activity Profile," in *Mirrors for Behavior.* Vol. X. Edited by Anita Simon and E. Gil Boyer. Philadelphia: Research for Better Schools, 1970.

Lindvall, C. M. *et al.* "Manual for IPI Student Observational Form," in *Mirrors for Behavior.* Vol. III. Edited by Anita Simon and E. Gil Boyer. Philadelphia: Research for Better Schools, 1967.

Lipe, Dewey, Margaret T. Steen, and Thomas J. Quirk. "PLAN Student Observation Scale," in *Mirrors for Behavior.* Vol. B. Edited by Anita Simon and E. Gil Boyer. Philadelphia: Research for Better Schools Incorporated, 1970.

Neujahr, James L. "An Analysis of Teacher-Pupil Interactions when Instruction Is Individualized." Unpublished Ed.D. dissertation, Teachers College, Columbia University, 1970.

Resnick, Lauren B. "Teacher Behavior in an Informal British Infant School." *School Review.* Vol. LXXXI, No. 1 (November 1972), pp. 63–83.

Steen, Margaret T., Thomas J. Quirk, and Dewey Lipe. "PLAN Teacher Observational Scale," in *Mirrors for Behavior.* Vol. B. Edited by Anita Simon and E. Gil Boyer. Philadelphia: Research for Better Schools, 1970.

Weick, Karl E. "Systematic Observational Methods," in *The Handbook of Social Psychology.* Vol. II. 2d ed. revised. Edited by Gardner Lindzey and Elliot Aronson. Reading, Mass.: Addison-Wesley, 1968.

DATE DUE